THE

GRAND CANYON

INCLUDING SUNSET CRATER AND WUPATKI
NATIONAL MONUMENTS

A TRAVELER'S GUIDE

BY
JEREMY SCHMIDT

Free Wheeling Travel Guides
PO Box 7494
Jackson Hole, WY 83001 USA

Corrections and suggestions: Although every effort has been made to assure accuracy, conditions do change with time. Any corrections or suggestions for making this guide easier to use are welcome at the address below. A free, new edition will be sent to any person whose comments result in a useful change.

maps: Wendy Baylor
photos: Grand Canyon National Park
illustrations: Jocelyn Slack
design: Wendy Baylor and Jeremy Schmidt

ISBN 1–881480–00–3

HOW TO USE
THIS GUIDE

Thumb maps show location and coverage of main maps

Locator arrows

National park area is shaded

Margin indicators give next map page

Standard map symbols indicate facilities

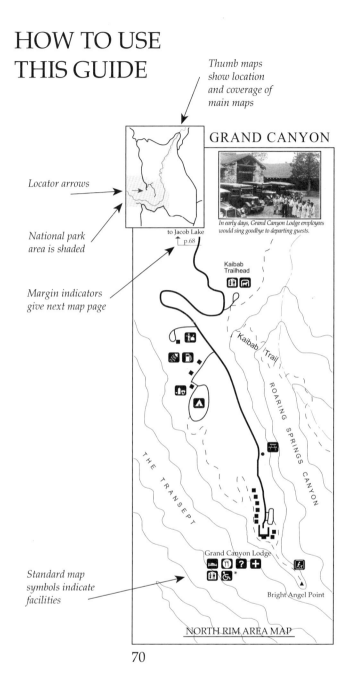

GRAND CANYON

In early days, Grand Canyon Lodge employees would sing goodbye to departing guests.

to Jacob Lake
↑ p.68

Kaibab Trailhead

Kaibab Trail

ROARING SPRINGS CANYON

THE TRANSEPT

Grand Canyon Lodge

Bright Angel Point

NORTH RIM AREA MAP

70

❑ Key maps inside front and back covers give page
   numbers for road maps.
❑ Index at the end of the book lists place names and
   subjects.
❑ Maps are generally in sequence, from south to north.
   Page numbers for adjoining maps are given in map
   margins. Or refer to thumb maps or key maps.
❑ This book is a guide for motorists, not hikers or other
   backcountry users, who will find topographic maps
   and trail guides essential.

Purple Prose For A Colorful Landscape

In the hundreds of books and thousands of articles written about it, the Grand Canyon has inspired much imaginative language. It's been called The Titan of Chasms; The Greatest Thing in the World; A New Wonder of the World; A Gash in Nature's Bared Breast. When confronted by what they described as "The Witchery of It All" and "Its Ineffable Beauty" (all of these from a promotional book published in 1906 by the Santa Fe Railroad), writers have consistently admitted defeat before launching into their own attempts.

One of the more ambitious comes from "A Gash in Nature's Bared Breast," by John L. Stoddard:

"The Grand Canyon of Arizona is Nature wounded unto death and lying stiff and ghastly, with a gash 200 miles in length and a mile in depth in her bared breast, from which is flowing fast a stream of life-blood called the Colorado... The globe itself seemed to have suddenly yawned asunder, leaving me trembling on the hither brink of two disseevered hemispheres... At my very feet, so near that I could have leaped at once into eternity, the earth was cleft to a depth of 6,600 feet — not by a narrow gorge like other canyons, but by an awful gulf within whose cavernous immensity the forests of the Adirondacks would appear like jackstraws, the Hudson Palisades would be an insignificant stratum, Niagara would be indiscernible, and cities could be tossed like pebbles."

John Muir was equally impressed but wrote with a better understanding of the natural processes: "It is the most tremendous expression of erosion and the most ornate and complicated I ever saw. Man seeks the finest marbles for sculptures; Nature takes cinders, ashes, sediments, and makes all divine in fineness of beauty — turrets, towers, pyramids, battlemented castles, rising in glowing beauty from the depths of this canyon of canyons noiselessly hewn from the smooth mass of the featureless plateau."

Contents

GRAND CANYON NATIONAL PARK

At first encounter, the Grand Canyon seems impossible. Standing on the edge, looking into that vast blue and red space, you see it all and you see nothing. The scale is too big for imagination, much less reality. The Colorado River, thundering in the bottom of the mile-deep gorge it has built, appears even through binoculars as a thin green ribbon. Visitors peering into the blue depths have been heard to say, "That little creek can't be the Colorado."

Yet from the rims to that "little creek," there lies so much more than open empty space. Rock formations tell a geologic story that began some two billion years ago. Intimate shaded side canyons drip with spring water and fill with the soft fragrance of wildflowers. Prehistoric dwellings appear well–preserved by the desert climate, although abandoned for 800 years or more. Deer, elk, bighorn sheep, mountain lions, coyotes and many other animals thrive at various levels in the canyon, along with more than 1500 species of plants, only two dozen of which are cacti. The Grand Canyon is far richer than it appears at first look, or even after many visits.

THE UNDERLYING STORY

The dominant theme of Grand Canyon is rock—rock in the most extraordinary shapes and colors, rock of enormous scale. Clearly, something important and unusual has happened here.

The story begins at the bottom of the Inner Gorge, where the Colorado River cuts through the black Vishnu Schist, a hard metamorphic rock more than 1.7 billion years old. From this ancient basement rock, the story leads upward through time and younger rock layers.

Old hands at the canyon learn to recognize geologic strata like familiar friends, distinguishing them by color, hardness, texture, fossil content and other characteristics. The rocks are so distinct that people give directions according to the names of strata. "Where the trail hits the Hermit Shale..." they will say; or "Just at the base of the Redwall Limestone...."

Rock types help determine the shape of the Canyon. For example, because Bright Angel Shale is relatively soft it forms slopes of rubble, in contrast to the harder cliff-forming Muav Limestone, or the even harder meta-morphics of the inner gorge which erode slowly to form a sharp vee-shaped canyon. Having been introduced to the park's geology, one begins to decipher the reasons behind its remarkable form; then the Canyon loses some of its strangeness, but none of its wonder.

The River and the Canyon

Above all, the Grand Canyon is a geological event, an affair of rock types, earth movement, deposition, and erosion. At the heart of the Canyon, and at the center of its story, flows the Colorado River. By understanding the river and its origins, we begin to understand the Canyon.

This is no simple matter. The river performs an apparent impossibility. From Lees Ferry for about 60 miles it flows south along the base of the Kaibab Plateau — until suddenly it changes course and cuts westward, slicing through the core of the uplifted highland. Rivers normally flow away from high ground, not through it.

Trying to explain this odd behavior continues to challenge geologists. Once it was thought that the river was very old, and that it carved the Canyon as the land rose beneath it. In other words, it pre-existed the uplift. New evidence, however, shows that the river began flowing in its present course through the Canyon only about five and a half million years ago; by that time the land was already near its modern elevation.

One current theory has gained wide acceptance. At the risk of oversimplifying this complex series of events, the story involves two rivers, one flowing into the Gulf of California, steadily eroding the highlands near its source, extending its reach toward the northeast. This is now the lower Colorado River, forming the border between California and Arizona. The second river, relatively small, followed the course of the upper Canyon, but the Canyon was not yet in existence. Instead, this second river wandered through a broad, gentle valley curving around the Kaibab Plateau and eventually draining northwest into the area which is now Nevada.

An important change happened when the lower river, clawing into the high plateau, breached a critical divide and captured its neighbor. The two rivers joined to become a single powerful stream, cutting rapidly downward. By this theory, the major work of cutting the Canyon was done in less than five million years and perhaps as little as three million.

LIFE ZONES

The shape of the land—its elevation, sun exposure, soil types, moisture content, slope and so forth—determines what lives upon it. In the Grand Canyon, habitats, like geological strata, fall into distinct elevational zones.

Beginning on the North Rim, the first habitat is called the Boreal Life Zone. Above 8,000 feet, this is a montane environment characterized by aspen, spruce and fir trees, and deep winter snow. Dropping into the canyon, we pass through a Transition Life Zone of pines, Gambel oak and mountain mahogany, giving way to pinyon-juniper woodland. The South Rim, which lies 1200 feet lower than the North Rim, is firmly within this zone. Travelers will recognize it as the classic woodland community of the high desert.

At around 5,000 feet begins the Upper Sonoran Life Zone, characterized by blackbrush scrub, yucca, agave, Mormon tea and various cacti. The heart of this zone is the Tonto Platform, a broad shelf on either side of the river. Cut like a ragged gash in the platform is the Inner Gorge, dropping to around 2000 feet elevation, where plants and animals of the Lower Sonoran Life Zone make their homes.

Finally there is the riparian habitat of the Colorado River and its tributary streams, a vibrant world, unexpected in the desert. Water-loving plants such as cottonwoods and willows grow along the banks providing habitat for raccoons, skunks, ringtail cats, toads, tree frogs and others. The river itself is a complex world of fish, insects and water plants.

CANYON PEOPLE

Compared to the Grand Canyon's ancient natural history, its human history is brief but no less interesting. Artifacts have been found that date to between 3000 and 4000 years ago, probably left by semi-nomadic hunters and gatherers who wandered throughout the region. They were followed by Anasazi (called Hisat Sinom by their Hopi descendants), the same culture that built the famous cliff dwellings of Mesa Verde National Park. Tracing the paths of these vanished "Ancient Ones" is one of archeology's most compelling mysteries, and the source of much controversy. The spirit of those who came before—who called this place home—enriches any

Canyon experience. Nowhere else in America can one get such a strong sense of the land's long habitation.

Spanish members of the Coronado expedition first saw the Canyon in 1540. Since then, this epic landscape has attracted dreamers and eccentrics, scientists and adventurers. Among them was John Wesley Powell, the one-armed geologist who led the first recorded descent of the Colorado River. In addition, miners, ranchers, road builders and rustlers have played their parts. The national park was established in 1919, but the human story continues to unfold in the form of modern issues: air pollution that sometimes shrouds the Canyon; uranium mining on the periphery; motorized travel on the river and in the air; and the growing impact of Glen Canyon Dam, which lies upstream of the park and controls the Colorado River.

Split twig figurines, found in Grand Canyon caves, seem to have had ceremonial functions — perhaps to bring good luck in hunting.

FALLING ROCKS

Rock falls continually in the canyon; occasionally in large masses that break off the canyon walls, leaving light-colored patches on cliffs, and rubble strewn across slopes below — dramatic evidence that the process of canyon building continues.

It would be natural to think of a rock avalanche as a momentary event, a sudden collapse. However, studies show that rockfall is a slow process. A single flake might slowly, almost imperceptibly, tilt outward for hundreds of years before reaching a point of critical instability until it gives way in a violent crash — like the Leaning Tower of Pisa, heading inexorably for a fall.

On the morning of August 13, 1934, visitors once experienced a rockfall beneath their very feet: "A sudden roar and a trembling of the foundation of Yavapai Observation Station advertised the presence of a rock slide below. A few seconds later dust began rising in vast quantities on the Canyon side of the station, first white then changing with astonishing rapidity to cream color and then red. For about a minute and a half the Canyon was almost totally obscured... a heavy layer of dust over the glass cases and chairs in the station remained as witness to the event... A column of rock approximately 150 feet high, 20 feet wide and 6 feet thick had collapsed." (Grand Canyon Nature Notes, January 1935).

TRAVELERS' INFORMATION

VISITOR CENTERS

Grand Canyon National Park visitor centers and museums provide brochures, books, maps, and general information. A free park newspaper, *The Guide*, is distributed at entrance stations and lists services, seasonal schedules, and hours of operation. Separate editions are available for the North and South rims.

On the South Rim, the main visitor center is in Grand Canyon Village. Nearby, at Yavapai Point, the Yavapai Museum features geological exhibits, along with a panoramic view of the Canyon. About 20 miles east, the Tusayan Museum has archeological displays adjacent to a prehistoric ruin. There is also a Visitor Information Center at Desert View, open seasonally.

On the North Rim, a National Park Service information desk is located in the lobby of the Grand Canyon Lodge.

Correspondence and requests for general information may be directed to park headquarters: Grand Canyon National Park, P.O. Box 129, Grand Canyon, AZ 86023 (tel: 602-638-7888).

ENTRANCE FEES

Entrance fees are $10 per private vehicle and all its passengers, with one permit valid for up to seven days. Individual travelers entering by other means (including bicycle, motorcycle, foot, bus, etc.) may obtain a $4 seven-day permit.

For $15, an annual permit allows unlimited visits to both rims for a calendar year; it includes the pass holder and immediate family or all passengers in a private vehicle. A Golden Eagle Pass, good in all national parks, costs $25 per calendar year. Finally, Golden Age Passports (for persons 62 or older) and Golden Access Passports (for handicapped persons) are free; these include not just park admission but reduced camping fees at National Park Service campgrounds also.

SEASON

The South Rim is open all year, although some facilities close and hours are cut back during the winter.

The North Rim is closed each winter, beginning with the first heavy snowfall (usually late October or early November) and lasting until mid-May. Early and late visitors should call ahead for conditions.

DRIVING

Both sides of the Canyon — especially the higher North Rim — are subject to storms at any time of year. Summer thunderstorms, although short-lived, can be fierce, bringing hail and lightning. Early and late in the season, visitors to the North Rim should be prepared for snow and slippery conditions.

WEST RIM DRIVE

During summer, from about Memorial Day to September 30, the 8-mile long West Rim Drive is closed to private vehicles (permits for disabled persons are available at the Visitor Center). Instead, free shuttle buses carry visitors back and forth. Although you must travel without the convenience of your personal car, this arrangement has its advantages. Without traffic, the rim is a more peaceful place; on calm days, you can hear birds singing far below the rim and free from the roar of motors. The buses also make it possible to combine walking with riding. The Rim Trail (beginning to the east at Yavapai Point) is paved to Maricopa Point, and extends all the way to Hermits Rest.

Restrooms and drinking water are found only at the end of the road, Hermits Rest. Watch your hat at overlooks. Sudden breezes catch people by surprise.

HIKING

There is no more rewarding way to see the Canyon than by walking on trails, either along the rim or into the Canyon itself. However, keep in mind that hiking here is very different from hiking in forests or mountains. There is little water and, in summer, intense heat. Going down is easy; coming back up is not. The Canyon has a way of drawing hikers ever deeper, until they are tired and their water is gone, and they face the long haul back to the rim. As a rule, even experienced walkers tend to be over-ambitious. It is best to set modest goals; consult with park rangers; and choose well-traveled trails (for example, the Kaibab or the Bright Angel) for one's first forays.

Permits are required for overnight camping in the Grand Canyon backcountry. The permits are free but limited. During the high season (April through October) backcountry campsites on the major trails are fully booked. Write to the park well in advance of your intended trip to request reservations. These may be obtained any time after October 1, covering the following calendar year. You may call for information and a backcountry planning kit at (602) 638-7888, or write to the Backcountry Reservations Office, P.O. Box 129, Grand Canyon, AZ 86023. Equipment can be rented at Babbitt's General Store in Grand Canyon Village

This book is not meant to be a hiking guide, nor is the following advice comprehensive. However, some basic rules are worth stating. 1) Carry water, up to two gallons per person per day, and learn about water sources along the trail. 2) Consider how much time you'll need for a given hike, and then double it. 3) Avoid hiking in the heat of the day. 4) Protect your skin and eyes from sun. 5) Wear light but supportive footwear; on the heavily traveled corridor trails (Bright Angel, South Kaibab, and North Kaibab), mountain boots are an unnecessary burden. 6) Carry food, including some emergency extras. 7) Stay on trails. What looks like a shortcut will almost never turn out to be one. 8) Pack light but don't forget safety items like a first aid kit, signal mirror and a flashlight. 9) When in doubt, check with a ranger before attempting any trail.

MULE RIDING

Mule trains, carrying passengers or freight, are an old tradition in the Canyon. They provide an alternative to hiking, but even riding a mule can feel like a strenuous activity. Day trips are available from both rims. From the South Rim, two-day trips go all the way to the Colorado River, spending the night at historic Phantom Ranch; bookings should be made up to a year in advance. For information, call (602) 638-2631 or 638-2401.

AIR TOURS

Sightseeing tours by helicopter and fixed-wing aircraft leave from numerous regional locations. Nearest to the Canyon are the heli pads in Tusayan and the adjacent Grand Canyon Airport outside the park. A list of air tour companies can be had at visitor centers.

RIVER TRIPS

Seeing the Canyon from river level provides a new, adventurous perspective on the deep wilderness that comprises most of the park. More than 20 companies operate trips taking five days to longer than two weeks. The only one-day trips run the smooth water of Glen Canyon above Lees Ferry, originating via Page, Arizona. A list of river companies is available at visitor centers.

HANDICAPPED ACCESS

Many overlooks and some trails on both rims are wheelchair accessible or accessible with assistance. In this guide, some are marked with a wheelchair symbol. An Accessibility Guide, along with permits for parking and access to the West Rim Drive are available at the Visitor Center.

SAFETY

The rim can be a dangerous place. When standing or walking at cliff edges, caution is a necessity. Exposure to heights causes dizziness in some people. Although most viewpoints have protective guardrails or stone walls, they are not childproof. At undeveloped points on the rim, there is a temptation to go farther out for better views, but loose stones and tree roots can make footing treacherous. Be careful with children; pets must be kept on a leash.

During thunderstorm season (July through September) lightning can be a hazard in exposed locations, even when the center of the storm is some distance away. Electricity crackling in the air is a warning to find shelter.

LODGING

Accommodations are available on both rims and in surrounding communities, including Tusayan near the South Rim and Jacob Lake 45 miles north of the North Rim. To watch sunset or dawn over the Grand Canyon is one of the greatest pleasures of visiting the park. This means staying overnight, which requires advance planning. During much of the year, Grand Canyon lodging is usually full. Reservations, made as early as possible, are essential. If no rooms are available, it's a long drive back to neighboring cities.

All South Rim lodging (including Phantom Ranch which is accessible only by foot and mule) is operated by Grand Canyon National Park Lodges. Contact them at P.O. Box 699, Grand Canyon, Arizona 86023 (tel: 602-638-2401). In Tusayan, try the Best Western Grand Canyon Squire Inn (602-638-2681); Moqui Lodge (602-638-2401); Quality Inn (602-638-2673); Red Feather (602-638-2414); and Seven-Mile Lodge (602-638-2291). For North Rim, contact TW Recreational Services, Box 400, Cedar City, Utah 84720 (tel: 801-586-7686).

CAMPGROUNDS

Park service campgrounds on both rims provide basic services, including tent pads, picnic tables, toilets, drinking water and trash collection. They include:

Mather Campground at Grand Canyon Village. Fee, $10 per night. Reservations up to eight weeks in advance available through MISTIX, at P.O. Box 85705, San Diego, CA 92138-5705 (tel: 800-365-2267); no reservations between December 1 and March 1. Showers, laundry and dump station are located nearby.

Desert View Campground, near the east entrance. No reservations, no hook-ups, and closed during winter. Fee, $8 per night.

North Rim Campground, on the North Rim. Fee, $10 per night. Reservations can be had through MISTIX (see above). No hook-ups, closed in winter. Shower, laundry and camper store located nearby.

Hook-ups can be had at **Trailer Village**, on the South Rim near Mather Campground. Open all year, operated by Grand Canyon National Park Lodges. Reservations: (602) 638-2401.

Outside the park, campsites are available at Babbitt's **Camper Village** in Tusayan. Open all year, hook-ups and other services. Call (602) 638-2887. The Kaibab National Forest offers simple camping at **Ten-X Campground** just south of Tusayan, **Demotte Campground** 16 miles north of the North Rim, and **Jacob Lake Campground** 45 miles north of the North Rim.

Glen Canyon National Recreation Area operates a campground at Lees Ferry on the Colorado River.

PETS

Pets are permitted on leash, and only on or near paved roads; never in the backcountry, on nature trails or in buildings. Kennel services are located in Grand Canyon Village on the South Rim (tel: 602-638-2631, ext. 6549).

EMERGENCIES

From pay phones call 911; from hotel and motel rooms, dial 9-911.

Medical facilities: On the **South Rim**, the Grand Canyon Clinic (638-2551 or 638-2469) provides routine care during business hours, and 24-hour emergency care. There is a pharmacy (638-2460) and a dentist (638-2395); for hours of operation, check the park newspaper. On the **North Rim**, a clinic is staffed by a Nurse Practitioner (638-2611); again, check the park newspaper for hours.

FURTHER READING AND SOURCE MATERIAL

Bookstores and other shops throughout the region carry a good selection of Grand Canyon publications. Within the park, several outlets are operated by the Grand Canyon Natural History Association, a non-profit organization donating its proceeds to park interpretive activities. A mail order catalog is available. Their address: P.O. Box 399, Grand Canyon, Arizona 86023 (tel: 602-638-2481).

Babbitt, Bruce. *Grand Canyon, An Anthology*, Northland Press, 1978

Beus, Stanley S. and Morales, Michael, editors. *Grand Canyon Geology*, Oxford University Press, 1990

Brown, Carothers and Johnson. *Grand Canyon Birds*, Univ. of Arizona, 1987

Carothers, Steven W. and Brown, Bryan T. *The Colorado River Through Grand Canyon*, Univ. of Arizona, 1991

Chronic, Halka. *Roadside Geology of Arizona*, Mountain Press, 1983

Foster, Lynne. *Exploring the Grand Canyon*, Grand Canyon Natural History Ass'n, 1990 (Juvenile audience)

Hughes, Donald J. *In the House of Stone and Light, A Human History of the Grand Canyon*, Grand Canyon Natural History Association, revised in 1988

Lavender, David. *River Runners of Grand Canyon,* Grand Canyon Natural History Ass'n, 1985

Phillips and Richardson. *Grand Canyon Wildflowers*, Grand Canyon Natural History Ass'n, 1990

Schullery, Paul, editor. *The Grand Canyon, Early Impressions*, Colorado Associated Univ. Press, 1981

Stegner, Wallace. *Beyond the Hundredth Meridian: John Wesley Powell and the Second Opening of the West*, Houghton Mifflin Co., 1953

Thybony, Scott. *Guide to Hiking the Inner Canyon*, Grand Canyon Natural History Ass'n, 1980

Thybony, Scott. *Fire and Stone, A Road Guide to Wupatki and Sunset Crater National Monuments*, Southwest Parks and Monuments Ass'n, 1987

Whitney, Stephen. *A Field Guide to the Grand Canyon*, Quill, 1982

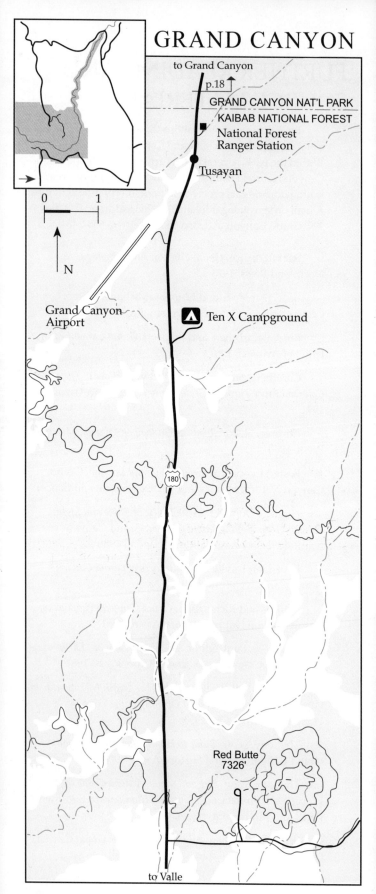

GRAND CANYON

to Grand Canyon

p.18

GRAND CANYON NAT'L PARK

KAIBAB NATIONAL FOREST

National Forest
Ranger Station

Tusayan

0   1

N

Grand Canyon
Airport

Ten X Campground

180

Red Butte
7326'

to Valle

First Glimpse of Grand Canyon

Just north of milepost 231, the North Rim is briefly visible, resembling a distant mesa of white stone partly covered with forest. It gives no hint that the greatest canyon on earth lies a few short miles ahead.

Side Roads

Although first-time visitors will undoubtedly head straight for the Canyon, those with time to spend and a wandering frame of mind can follow numerous side roads to places of interest in the Kaibab National Forest. The forest headquarters, providing maps and information, is located just north of Tusayan.

Ponderosa Pine

Around milepost 228, ponderosa pines intermingle with pinyon and juniper. Also called western yellow pine, ponderosa are recognized by their height, their large girth, and their long needles. On the Kaibab Plateau they live at elevations of 6,200 to 8,200 feet.

Kaibab Limestone

In contrast to the red sediments and the black volcanic rocks seen to the south, most of the surface here is made of light-colored stone: the fossil-filled Kaibab Limestone. Despite changes in elevation, and long distances, almost every mile of every road covered in this guide rests on Kaibab Limestone.

Red Butte

Named for its color, the butte is a remnant of soft mudstone formations that once covered this area, but eroded almost completely away. Red Butte is protected from erosion by a cap of hard volcanic lava. The Havasupai tribe claims it as a sacred place; it is now the site of a controversial uranium mining development.

Coconino Plateau

The road traverses gently sloping country; this is the southern edge of the Kaibab Upwarp, a great highland across which the Grand Canyon has been cut. On the other side of the Canyon, it is called the Kaibab Plateau. On this side, although it is really the same geographic feature, its name is the Coconino Plateau.

As the elevation increases, and the average temperatures grow cooler, the forest changes. Near the community of Valle there are almost no trees. A few miles north, pinyon pine and juniper dominate. Forming what is called "P-J," forest, these small but lovely trees cover the Kaibab Plateau between elevations of 5,500 and 6,800 feet.

A line of volcanic mountains is visible to the south, most notably the San Francisco Peaks near Flagstaff. Mt. Humphreys, the tallest, is 12,643 feet high and last erupted 400,000 to 600,000 years ago.

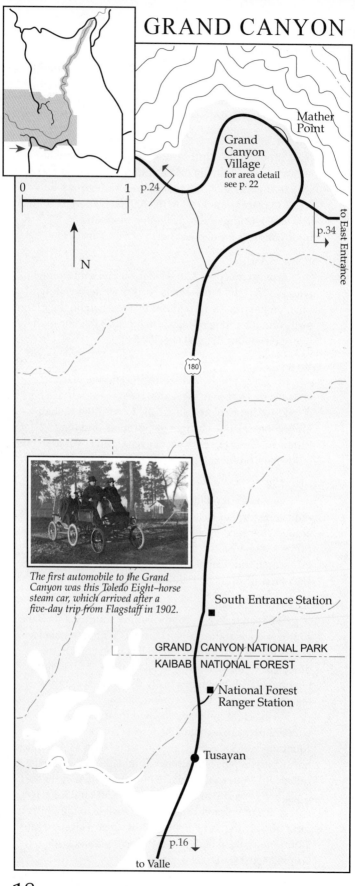

GRAND CANYON

Mather Point

Grand Canyon Village
for area detail
see p. 22

p.24

p.34 to East Entrance

0   1

N

180

South Entrance Station

The first automobile to the Grand
Canyon was this Toledo Eight–horse
steam car, which arrived after a
five-day trip from Flagstaff in 1902.

GRAND   CANYON NATIONAL PARK

KAIBAB   NATIONAL FOREST

■ National Forest
Ranger Station

Tusayan

p.16

to Valle

GRAND CANYON VILLAGE

The village provides all necessary services: lodging, restaurants, fuel, groceries and supplies, medical care, and park information. For locations see the map on page 22; also check pages 10 through 14.

MATHER POINT

For many visitors this overlook provides the first full view of the Grand Canyon. Because there is nowhere else like it in the world, and because it opens so suddenly at one's feet, the first impression can last a lifetime.

The Grand Canyon is 277 miles long, and averages 4,000 to 5,000 feet in depth from the South Rim. At Mather Point, the North Rim stands 10 miles away and about 1000 feet higher. As big as it seems, keep in mind that only a small part of the canyon is visible from Mather Point: about one-third of its length, and only a hint of its hidden complexity. It can take years and much effort to develop a full understanding of this unique landscape. As familiarity increases, details gradually fill in the blank spaces in one's mind. The Tonto Platform, for example, the flat-looking, greenish ledge seen far below on both sides of the river, is not as flat as it appears, nor is it barren. It is home to many creatures and plants, only a few of which are cacti and rattlesnakes. But without actually being on the Tonto, it is hard to get a sense of the place. The Canyon holds many secrets, more than any one person can ever know.

SOUTH ENTRANCE STATION

Admission to Grand Canyon National Park requires a permit, available at this and other entrance stations. See page 10 for a description of fees and types of permits. Also available here are introductory maps and The Guide, a free park publication with informative articles and a listing of interpretive programs. For more detailed information, stop at the Visitor Center at Grand Canyon Village.

Before roads and cars, people came to the canyon by horse-drawn stage, a two-day trip from Flagstaff. When the railroad was finished in 1901, travel became much smoother. The first auto—a Toledo Eight-horse steam car—struggled to the South Rim in 1902, more a stunt than a demonstration of improved traveling techniques. The journey took five days and involved considerable walking on the part of the four passengers. But if anyone scoffed back then, they were eating their words by 1926, when more visitors came by auto than by rail.

TUSAYAN

Most visitor services are available in Tusayan, including restaurants, shops, air tours, and camping. Kaibab National Forest headquarters, providing maps and other information on the surrounding area, is about one-half mile north of town.

THE VIEW FROM YAVAPAI POINT

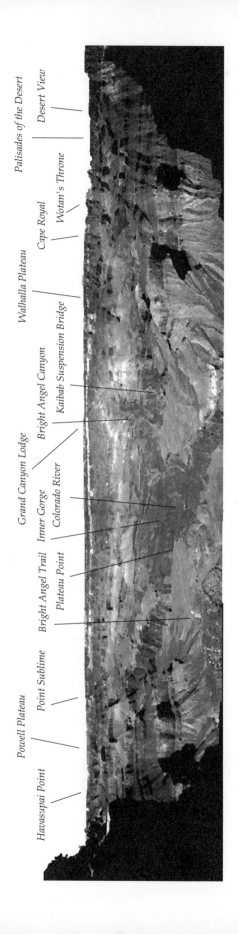

Havasupai Point · Powell Plateau · Point Sublime · Bright Angel Trail · Plateau Point · Grand Canyon Lodge · Inner Gorge · Colorado River · Bright Angel Canyon · Kaibab Suspension Bridge · Walhalla Plateau · Cape Royal · Wotan's Throne · Palisades of the Desert · Desert View

YAVAPAI POINT PANORAMA

A short walk leads to a series of viewpoints and a museum that provides a good introduction to the Canyon and its geologic history. Perched on the rim, the museum also offers a sheltered viewing platform during storms. A wide stretch of the Canyon is visible, from Palisades of the Desert 18 miles (29km) east to Great Thumb Mesa, 30 miles (48km) northwest.

From here, only glimpses of the Colorado River are seen; one view includes the Kaibab suspension bridge, appearing as the merest thread strung over the water. Also at river level, the green foliage of cottonwood trees marks Phantom Ranch. Behind it, incised deeply into the North Rim, Bright Angel Canyon follows the Bright Angel Fault.

Look for the South Kaibab Trail on the red ridge just to the east. Hikers can reach Phantom Ranch and the Colorado River by two trails, the Bright Angel or the South Kaibab. Hiking time down is about four hours. Coming back up, which is not recommended on the same day as descending, takes up to twice as long.

Other prominent sights include the trail to Plateau Point some 3,100 feet (950 meters) below, from which hikers and mule riders obtain a good view of the Colorado River and the inner canyon.

It is a very different world at the bottom of the Canyon, where conditions are similar to those found in southern Arizona.

Early visitors on the banks of the Colorado River near Phantom Ranch.

Temperatures are much warmer. On a day in May, the South Rim might see a high of 78 degrees Fahrenheit (25°C) and a low of 36 (2°C), while at Phantom Ranch the high is 98 (37°C) and the low 73 (23°C). Despite the high summer temperatures, the river and numerous permanent streams support trout and beaver and other water-loving creatures. During winter, snow covers both rims but it rarely freezes at river level.

RIM TRAIL

This pleasant foot path stretches from Yavapai Museum through Grand Canyon Village all the way to Hermits Rest; it's paved for its first 3½ miles (5.6 km) to Maricopa Point. Walking even a short part of this easy path is a good way to break the routine of motorized touring. During summer months, when the shuttle is operating, one popular idea is to walk for a distance, then ride the bus back to your starting point.

21

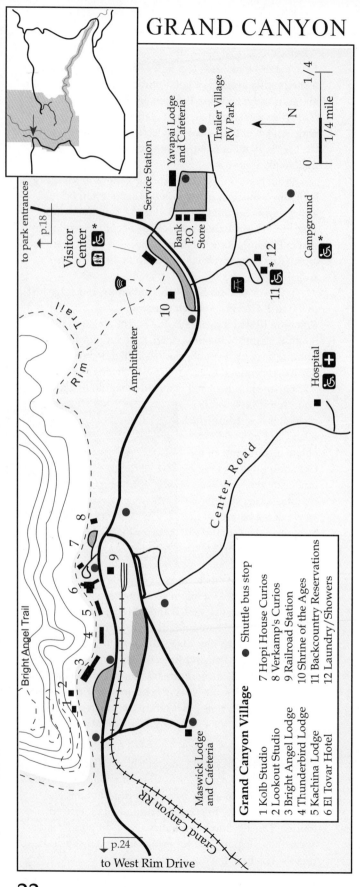

GRAND CANYON

Grand Canyon Village

1 Kolb Studio
2 Lookout Studio
3 Bright Angel Lodge
4 Thunderbird Lodge
5 Kachina Lodge
6 El Tovar Hotel

7 Hopi House Curios
8 Verkamp's Curios
9 Railroad Station
10 Shrine of the Ages
11 Backcountry Reservations
12 Laundry/Showers

● Shuttle bus stop

p.18
p.24

GRAND CANYON VILLAGE

The village grew up around the railhead, with the El Tovar Hotel, completed in 1905, as its centerpiece. There are many other historic buildings and points of interest clustered along the Canyon's rim, all of them best seen by walking. During summer, free shuttle buses operate through the village and along the West Rim Drive.

INFORMATION

The best source of information is the Visitor Center, with its museum displays, media programs and publication sales. Rangers are on duty to answer questions and make suggestions. Open daily; hours vary with season.

The El Tovar

HISTORIC STRUCTURES

Perched on the rim stands the historic **El Tovar Hotel**, built in 1905 for a leisure-class clientele. In the early years, it was common for people to stay weeks and even months at a time. Coats and ties were worn at dinner; after which one could head for roulette and craps tables in the basement saloon. The El Tovar is still a fashionable if less formal setting and worth a visit even for non-guests.

Also on the rim is the **Bright Angel Lodge**, where a small museum tells the story of early tourism in the days of steam trains, stage coaches, and "Harvey Girls." The lodge was designed by Mary E. J. Colter, an architect attracted to indigenous themes. Colter also designed **Desert View Watchtower** and **Hermits Rest** (both located outside the village) and **Lookout Studio**, a structure that demonstrates how buildings can blend into Canyon surroundings. Perhaps her most fanciful effort was **Hopi House**, adjacent to the El Tovar. Wanting a new structure that looked old, she borrowed ideas from the Hopi mesa towns east of the Canyon. In early days, Hopis were invited to live there as a sort of cultural exhibit. Today, Hopi House is both a curio shop and a curiosity. Also of interest is the **Kolb Studio**, former home and business of photographers Emery and Ellsworth Kolb; it now houses a bookstore whose proceeds will help fund its rehabilitation.

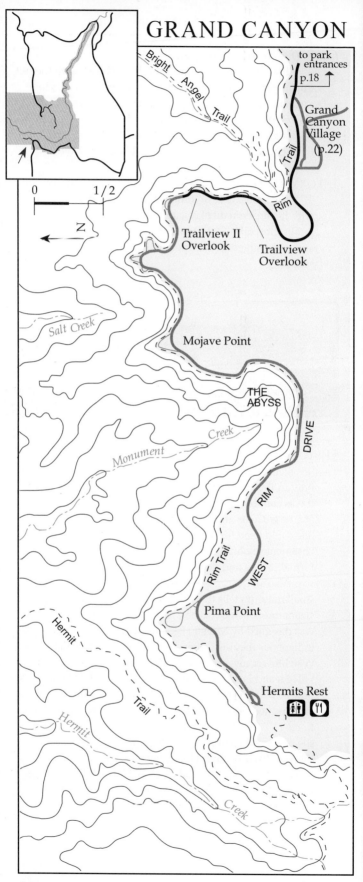

GRAND CANYON

to park
entrances
p.18

Grand
Canyon
Village
(p.22)

Bright Angel Trail

Rim Trail

Trailview II
Overlook

Trailview
Overlook

Mojave Point

THE
ABYSS

Salt Creek

Creek

Monument

DRIVE

RIM

Rim Trail

WEST

Pima Point

Hermit

Trail

Hermit

Hermits Rest

Creek

0   1/2

N

WEST RIM DRIVE

This popular 8-mile drive ends at Hermits Rest after passing numerous viewpoints. **Note:** in summer, the road is closed to private vehicles. For information about free shuttle buses and other details, see page 11.

The drive begins just west of the Bright Angel Lodge, at an overlook. The overlook marks the top of the Bright Angel Fault, a break in the rock where earth movements forced a 186-foot (57m) displacement. The fault accounts for the side canyon down which the Bright Angel Trail leads; it also explains why the rim is higher to the west. The prominent drainage across the river cutting deep into the North Rim is called Bright Angel Canyon. Long and straight, it follows the same prominent fault.

The West Rim Drive was built by the Santa Fe Railroad in 1910 to 1912, and used by open-topped tourist stages; until 1919, no autos were permitted. Back then, tickets cost $3 for the round-trip to Hermits Rest. Today, when shuttle buses are running, the trip is free.

TRAILVIEW OVERLOOK

The road climbs the higher side of the Bright Angel Fault and rejoins the rim at this overlook, named for its view of the Bright Angel Trail. A short concrete walkway leads to two viewpoints.

The Bright Angel Trail began as an Indian route to the generous springs at Indian Garden, following one of the few natural paths into the Canyon. In the late 1800s, miners improved the ancient route to permit pack animals to make the journey. One of the miners, Ralph Cameron, operated the trail as a toll road for nearly 20 years. He monopolized access through mining claims at strategic points; these were finally invalidated and the trail became public property.

A good portion of the trail is visible from the lower viewpoint. Tiny figures can be seen climbing the unrelenting switchbacks far below. It is interesting to note how the color of the trail changes as it passes through various rock strata on its 9-mile journey from rim to river. Indian Garden (the bright patch of cottonwoods) is 3,100 vertical feet down; all the way to the Colorado River at Phantom Ranch (not visible from here) is 4,400 feet.

For walkers seeking an easier path, the foot trail from here to Maricopa Point is relatively flat and paved—a pleasant, scenic stroll.

TRAILVIEW II

Here is another view of the Bright Angel Trail, for those who cannot or prefer not to walk the steps down to Trailview Point.

25

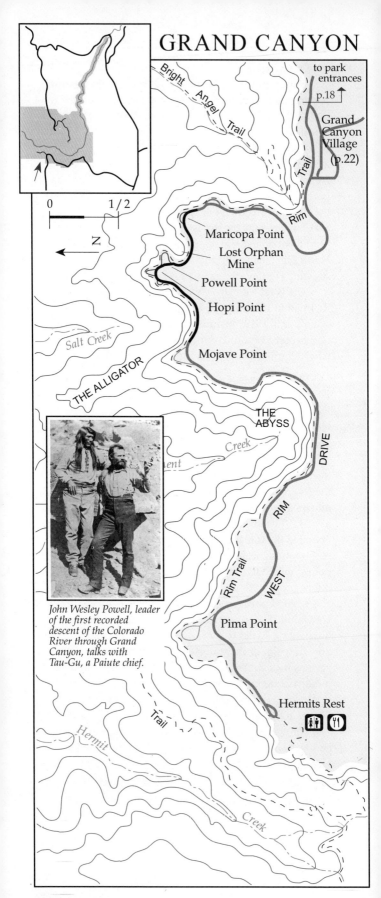

GRAND CANYON

to park entrances
p.18 →

Grand Canyon Village (p.22)

Bright Angel Trail

Rim Trail

Maricopa Point
Lost Orphan Mine
Powell Point
Hopi Point

Salt Creek

Mojave Point

THE ALLIGATOR

THE ABYSS

Creek

____ent

RIM DRIVE

Rim Trail

WEST

Pima Point

John Wesley Powell, leader of the first recorded descent of the Colorado River through Grand Canyon, talks with Tau-Gu, a Paiute chief.

Hermit

Trail

Hermits Rest

Creek

0   1/2

Z ←

MARICOPA POINT

Just west of Maricopa Point stands the tram tower of Lost Orphan Mine, a copper mine established in 1893. In the 1950s and 60s it produced uranium, and is now inactive.

Straight below the overlook, Horn Canyon cuts down to the river and the inner gorge, where pink ribbons of Zoroaster Granite marble the smooth black Vishnu Schist. This is hard rock, the basement rock of the Grand Canyon, more than 1.7 billion years old.

The Canyon plays visual tricks. Although it looks as if you should see the Colorado River at the bottom of Horn Canyon, it is hidden by intervening and deceptive walls of schist. The prominent ridge of red stone below and to the right is called The Battleship; it catches nice sunset light.

POWELL POINT

A monument here honors John Wesley Powell, the one-armed geologist and explorer who led the first successful traverse of the Colorado River through Grand Canyon in 1869 and again in 1871–72. These expeditions were two of many accomplishments for this talented man. Powell influenced the scientific exploration of the country, first as a scientist, then as director of both the Bureau of American Ethnology and the US Geological Survey. The river he ran, however, is invisible from here.

HOPI POINT

Some of the South Rim's most expansive views can be had from this point, which is a good choice for sunset viewing. Far to the east, the horizon is formed by Palisades of the Desert, where the Colorado River turns the corner and begins its great work of cutting through the Kaibab Plateau. The river itself can be seen here in short stretches, including the tail end of Granite Rapid.

The long red promontory just to the west, called The Alligator, is made of Supai Group strata, topped and stained by Hermit Shale. Most of the shale and all the overlying layers have eroded off. It is amazing to consider that most of this erosion has happened within the last 5.5 million years. The canyon rocks are ancient, up to 1.7 billion years old, but the Grand Canyon itself is a relatively recent creation.

Like a shelf deep in the Canyon, the Tonto Platform is easily seen from here but reached only with difficulty. It looks flat, as if walking along it should be easy, but this is an illusion. The Tonto Trail, visible as a fine line along the edge of the Inner Gorge, winds and meanders. It takes hikers a long time to go a short distance. The green color is partly due to the rock, but mostly to the desert scrub that grows there. There are fewer trails on the north side of the river, making that area even more remote and unvisited.

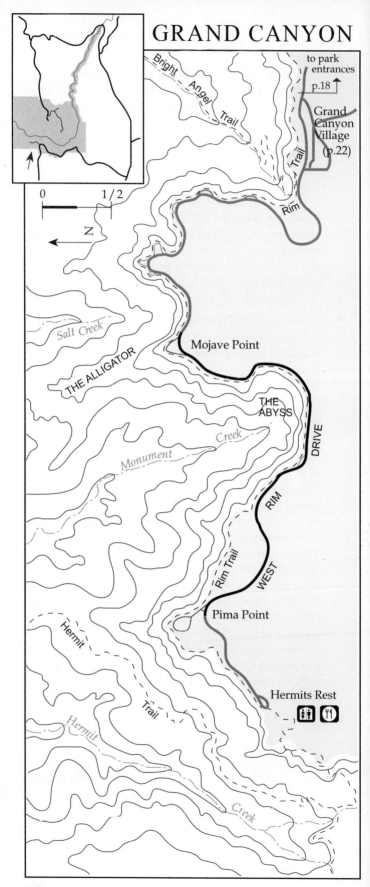

GRAND CANYON

to park entrances p.18

Grand Canyon Village (p.22)

Bright Angel Trail

Rim Trail

0   1/2

N

Salt Creek

THE ALLIGATOR

Mojave Point

THE ABYSS

Creek

Monument

RIM

DRIVE

Rim Trail

WEST

Pima Point

Hermit

Trail

Hermit

Hermits Rest

Creek

MOHAVE POINT

Hermit Rapid, prominent on the river to the west, is a classic constriction rapid, the most common type in Grand Canyon. Squeezed between the canyon wall and debris washed out of tributaries, the river channel is pinched, resulting in turbulence. In this case, flash floods roaring down Hermit Canyon have spilled huge boulders, gravel, and sand into the river. As the river forces its way over the debris, some of its biggest waves are formed.

Upstream from Hermit Rapid the tail end of Granite Rapid is visible; the upper, more gnarly stretch is hidden behind the red promontory called The Alligator.

Over the 277-mile length of the canyon, the Colorado drops 2000 feet (610m); there are 160 major rapids, the biggest being Crystal Rapid and Lava Falls.

ARCHEOLOGY NOTE

With binoculars, you can sometimes find small stone and clay structures under overhangs not far below the rim. These were used by prehistoric people for storage of corn and other crops. The rim would obviously be an attractive place to live, but why would people build storage structures in such inaccessible places? It took real effort to get down there, probably climbing down a break in the cliffs and then traversing along steep slopes for long distances. It would have been easier to move along the ledges when snow covered the rim; at those times, water would be abundant, and firewood was in good supply, but you still wonder what they were doing there. The only reason people today have for going there is to investigate the artifacts of the ancient culture.

THE ABYSS

The road edges dizzyingly close to a great curved cliff nearly 3,000 feet high. Several overlooks in the next few miles provide chances to peer into the Canyon's depths. Monument Creek, which drains The Abyss, takes its name from several stone towers; the largest of these stands visible in the middle of the creekbed where it begins cutting a sharp gorge through the Tonto Platform. Where the creek meets the Colorado, its erosion debris has caused a major rapid, Granite, which is visible from Pima Point.

THE VIEW FROM PIMA POINT

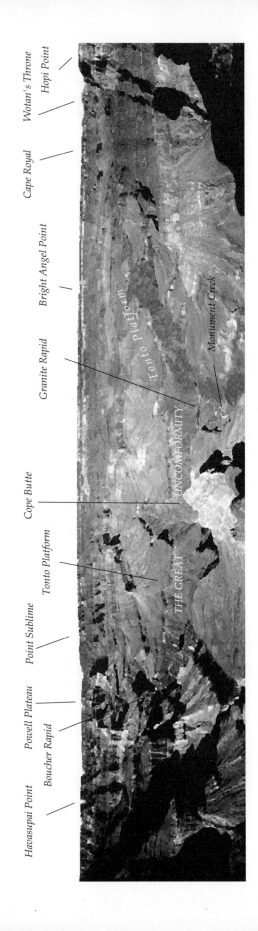

Havasupai Point
Boucher Rapid
Powell Plateau
Point Sublime
Tonto Platform
Cope Butte
Granite Rapid
Bright Angel Point
Cape Royal
Wotan's Throne
Hopi Point

Tonto Platform
Monument Creek
UNCOMFORMITY
THE GREAT

Panorama From Pima Point (Elev. 6798')

Projecting into the Canyon between Monument and Hermit creeks, Pima Point commands a broad panorama stretching from the Powell Plateau (26 miles west) to Cape Royal (15 miles east). From here there is a particularly good view of the Inner Gorge. Several stretches of the river are visible, including the lower half of Granite Rapid.

Canyon Islands

Standing separate from the distant North Rim are numerous buttes and pinnacles—erosional remnants called "temples" and "towers" by the mapmakers who named them. Biologists once speculated that different forms of plants or animals might have developed on the larger of these isolated points of land, as if they were islands in the sky, separated from events on the biological mainland. There was good reason to think this way. The Canyon has been a geographic and climatic barrier for long enough that some animals have developed distinct sub-species on its two rims. For example, consider the large tassel-eared squirrels that live in the ponderosa pine forest. On the North Rim, they have white tails and are called Kaibab squirrels while on the South Rim they have grey tails and are called Abert squirrels—different forms of one species.

In 1937, a well-publicized expedition sponsored by the American Museum of Natural History visited Shiva Temple and Wotan's Throne hoping to find other biologic differences. The scientists collected various rodents and noted the presence of deer antlers and Pueblo Indian artifacts but found no unusual evolutionary developments. Although erosion has isolated them from the main plateau, the "islands" support many of the same plants and animals that live on the neighboring rim.

The Great Unconformity

From the Canyon rim to the broad Tonto Platform, the layers of rock appear to be neatly stacked pages of a vast geologic history book. Actually there are some pages missing, and occasional disturbances caused by earth movements, but in general the story is remarkably well-preserved—up to the point where whole chapters have been torn out. This happened in the distant past, when rock layers which had been tilted, uplifted, and bent were then eroded flat, so that the layers resembled woodgrain in a planed board; the surface was smooth but underlying layers were not horizontal. Much time passed until there began another period of deposition, and the neatly sequenced strata that we stand on today were laid down on the old eroded surface. The point of contact, representing a large gap in the geologic story and called the Great Unconformity, is visible beneath the Tapeats Sandstone.

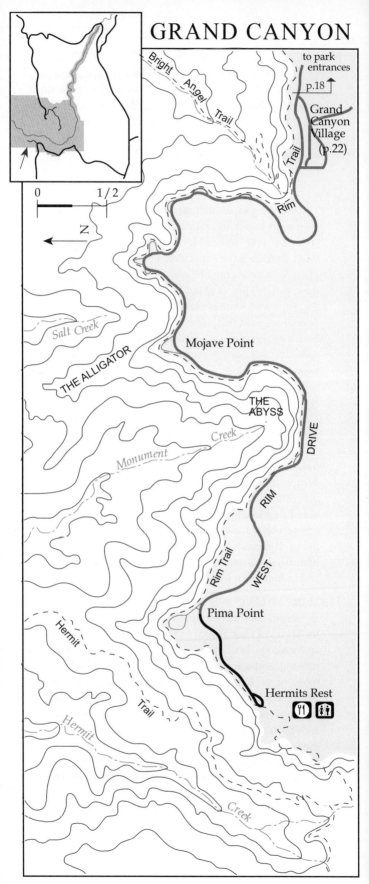

GRAND CANYON

to park
entrances
p.18 ↑

Grand
Canyon
Village
(p.22)

Bright — Angel — Trail

Rim Trail

Rim

0   1/2

← Z

Salt Creek

THE ALLIGATOR

Mojave Point

THE ABYSS

Creek

Monument

DRIVE

RIM

WEST

Rim Trail

Pima Point

Hermit

Trail

Hermit

Hermits Rest

Creek

The Hermit

Louis D. Boucher, a French-Canadian prospector, came to the Grand Canyon in the early 1890s. He was called a hermit not because of strong antisocial attitudes but because he lived and prospected in a remote corner of the Canyon. He made his home at a lovely oasis called Dripping Springs near the head of what came to be called Hermit Canyon. His copper mine was located one drainage farther west in Boucher Canyon. Never a great success at mining, he grew a famous fruit orchard and entertained occasional tourists; by 1912, he had moved to Utah, leaving behind little but his lonely nickname.

About that time the Santa Fe Railroad, irked by the fees charged on the private Bright Angel toll trail, obtained permission to build a new tourist route into the Canyon. Beginning on Boucher's old path (he called it the Silver Bell Trail) the new trail followed Hermit Canyon to Hermit Camp, a cluster of tent cabins 3,000 feet below the rim on the Tonto Platform. The camp closed in 1930 but the foundations are still visible.

Although the road ends at Hermits Rest, the Grand Canyon stretches many more miles, well beyond the western horizon. The volcanic mountains Emma and Trumbull, and the long escarpment of the Uinkaret Mountains, are barely visible nearly 60 miles away. Yet the distance from here to there represents roughly a third of the Canyon's total length.

Hermits Rest

An old New Mexican mission bell in a limestone arch greets visitors to Hermits Rest. This is the end of the West Rim Road and the beginning of the Hermit Trail. There are restrooms here; also a curio store and snack shop.

Hermits Rest was designed by Mary E. J. Colter, the same architect who designed Desert View Watchtower and other striking buildings along the South Rim. The building is a flight of fancy, made of native stone perched on the brink of the

The arch at Hermits Rest

Canyon, half buried by native soil and dominated by an enormous fireplace. From its comfortable shaded porch the western canyon stretches into the distance: a sea of pinnacles, buttes and mesas.

Here is also a clear view of Dripping Spring Canyon, where Louis Boucher, "The Hermit," lived around the turn of the century. It is an all-day hike to the springs and back, but a rewarding trail even if you go only part way.

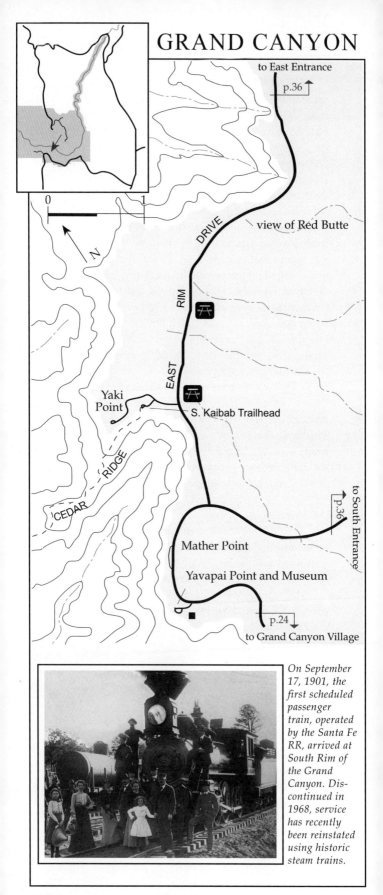

GRAND CANYON

to East Entrance

p.36

view of Red Butte

RIM DRIVE

EAST

N

0   1

Yaki Point

S. Kaibab Trailhead

CEDAR RIDGE

to South Entrance

p.36

Mather Point

Yavapai Point and Museum

to Grand Canyon Village

p.24

On September 17, 1901, the first scheduled passenger train, operated by the Santa Fe RR, arrived at South Rim of the Grand Canyon. Discontinued in 1968, service has recently been reinstated using historic steam trains.

YAKI POINT AND KAIBAB TRAILHEAD

One branch of this road, the left fork, ends at a parking area for the South Kaibab Trail. For better views of the Canyon, take the right fork and proceed to Yaki Point.

Yaki Point is one of the South Rim's quieter overlooks but it reveals an important element of the Grand Canyon story. Seen from here, the southwesterly slope of the Kaibab Plateau is distinctly visible. The slope explains why most water falling on the South Rim flows away from the Canyon, while on the North Rim, surface water drains into it. As a result, there is more erosion on the north side; tributary canyons are longer; and there are more permanent streams than on the South Rim.

Rain falling on the South Rim flows away from the Canyon. On the North Rim, water runs into the Canyon, causing more erosion and supporting more streams.

KAIBAB TRAIL VIEW

Here is a good view of the Kaibab Trail as it descends from near Yaki Point to a red saddle called Cedar Ridge which, strictly speaking, should instead be called Juniper Ridge. The trees that grow on the saddle, like those on the rim, do resemble cedars but are in fact Utah junipers. True cedars are native to Europe, not America.

YAVAPAI POINT

A short walk leads to a series of viewpoints and a museum that provides a good introduction to the Canyon and its geologic history. Perched on the rim, the museum also offers a sheltered viewing platform during storms. A wide stretch of the canyon is visible, from Palisades of the Desert in the east to Great Thumb Mesa in the northwest. (see panorama, page 20)

GRAND CANYON

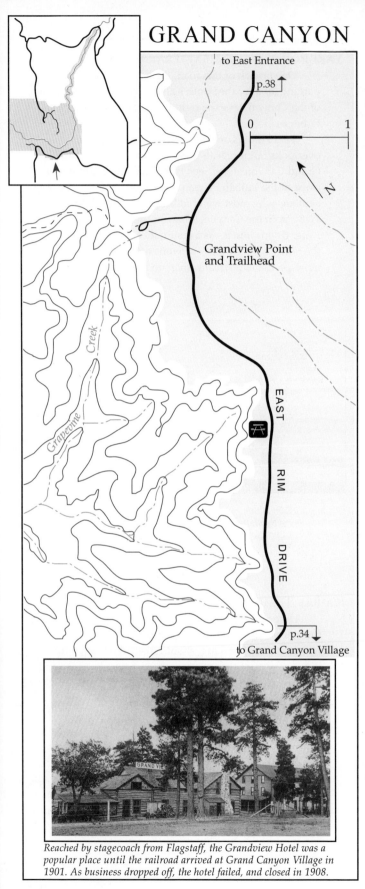

to East Entrance

p.38

0   1

N

Grandview Point
and Trailhead

EAST RIM DRIVE

Grapevine Creek

p.34
to Grand Canyon Village

Reached by stagecoach from Flagstaff, the Grandview Hotel was a popular place until the railroad arrived at Grand Canyon Village in 1901. As business dropped off, the hotel failed, and closed in 1908.

J. W. Thurber, who owned a stage line and the original Bright Angel Hotel, transporting tourists on the rim, c.1900.

NATURE NOTES

In shaded alcoves just below the Canyon rim grow conifers that are otherwise unseen in this area. These are Douglas fir, common at higher altitudes on the North Rim but limited here to shaded pockets where the air is cooler and the soil holds more moisture.

The situation on the North Rim, 1200 feet higher, is just the opposite. There, pinyon and juniper grow in a narrow strip along the rim, where the southern exposure and heated air welling up from the Canyon create a relatively warm microclimate.

GRAPEVINE CREEK

The road skirts the rim above Grapevine Canyon, which takes its name from dense tangles of wild grape that grow along the damp, spring-fed bottom. The vines drape cottonwood trees and various shrubs that also thrive there, giving the creekbed a lush, overgrown appearance.

The land at this point is higher than Grand Canyon Village, resulting in slightly cooler and wetter conditions that favor a different range of vegetation. Ponderosa pines grow tall, and grass is more plentiful, attracting grazing animals. Deer are often seen in morning and evening hours. Elk are also present but less common. From time to time, drivers report seeing mountain lions in this area.

CANYON BIRDS

Watch for birds cruising along the cliff edge. Violet-green swallows and white-throated swifts fly close to the rock cliffs. Often together, and about the same size, swallows and swifts can be hard to tell apart. The swallow has a completely white breast and a rounder body than the swift. The swift flies with an unusual twinkling motion of its wings, and generally flies faster than the swallow; some say swifts look like flying cigars because of their narrow tails.

Ravens are also commonly seen from the rim, often far out in the Canyon's gulf. Although black, their wings sometimes glint in the sun, making them appear as white as sea gulls. Aside from ravens, the most common soaring birds at Grand Canyon are vultures, as big as eagles but easily distinguished by their wobbly flight and their outstretched wings held in a broad dihedral, a wide vee. The wings of other soaring birds are held flat.

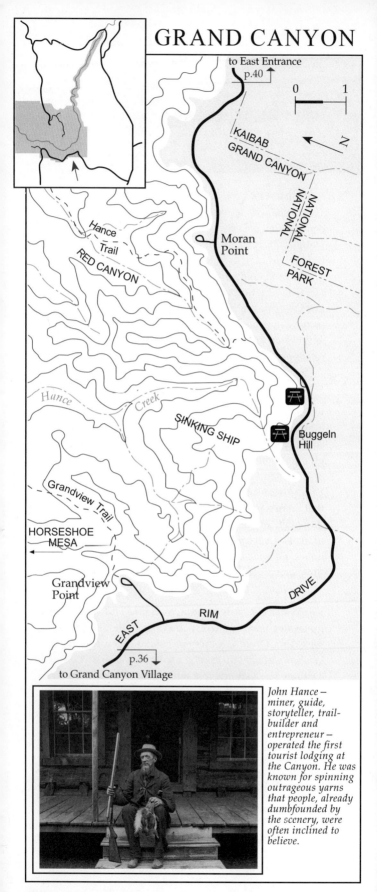

GRAND CANYON

to East Entrance
p.40

0   1

N

KAIBAB
GRAND CANYON

NATIONAL

NATIONAL

FOREST
PARK

Hance
Trail

RED CANYON

Moran
Point

Hance   Creek

SINKING SHIP

Buggeln
Hill

Grandview Trail

HORSESHOE
MESA

Grandview
Point

EAST   RIM   DRIVE

p.36
to Grand Canyon Village

John Hance —
miner, guide,
storyteller, trail-
builder and
entrepreneur —
operated the first
tourist lodging at
the Canyon. He was
known for spinning
outrageous yarns
that people, already
dumbfounded by
the scenery, were
often inclined to
believe.

MORAN POINT

Thought to be named for painter Thomas Moran, this point provides a fine view westward. Moran first gained attention as a member of the 1871 Hayden Expedition to Yellowstone; his astonishing watercolors, corroborated by photographs by William H. Jackson, influenced Congress in establishment of the world's first national park. His paintings of Grand Canyon also had an important effect. In early years, some people thought of the Canyon as forbidding and desolate, for all its size. Moran's paintings said yes, it is powerful, but also beautiful and worthy of artistic appreciation.

THE SINKING SHIP

One of the most interesting questions in Grand Canyon geology is how the Canyon came to be carved across a high plateau. Drainage systems usually flow away from high points, not through them. Visible from Moran Point lies part of the answer—a well-named formation called the Sinking Ship. Complete with superstructure, masts and bridge, its tilting layers are telltales of the Grandview Monocline, a fold in the otherwise horizontal rock layers that surround it. The Colorado River, as it carved its way around the Kaibab Plateau, would naturally have slipped farther and farther south, avoiding the high ground; but when it hit the Grandview monocline, a resistant "wall" of limestone, its southerly movement ended, and the river was forced to erode downward into what is now the Grand Canyon.

INNER GORGE

From Moran Point can be seen two different stretches of the river. Downstream, to the west, it flows deep within the hard black walls of the Inner Gorge, the ancient bedrock of the canyon. Upstream, it wanders more freely in broad bends through the soft, reddish sediments of the Grand Canyon Supergroup. The Canyon owes its shape and appearance largely to the characteristics of its rock. Hardness, mineral content, chemical composition, orientation, faulting, metamorphosis and other factors are all reflected in the resulting landscape.

GRANDVIEW POINT

This viewpoint is some 600 feet above Grand Canyon Village. Directly beneath the overlook, Horseshoe Mesa was the site of the Last Chance copper mine, established in 1890 by Pete Berry and two partners Niles and Ralph Cameron—the same fellows who justified their control of the Bright Angel Trail with mining claims that never produced ore. The Last Chance, however, was a legitimate mine. Despite the cost of hauling out every pound on mules, the ore was good enough (up to 70% pure copper) for the mine to keep operating until 1907. The old diggings remain a curiosity for hikers on the Grandview Trail.

GRAND CANYON

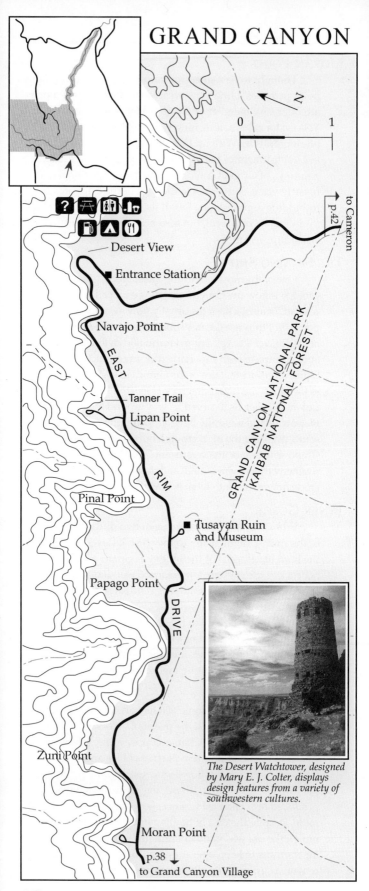

0   1

N

to Cameron
p.42

Desert View

Entrance Station

Navajo Point

EAST

Tanner Trail

Lipan Point

RIM

Pinal Point

Tusayan Ruin
and Museum

Papago Point

DRIVE

GRAND CANYON NATIONAL PARK

KAIBAB NATIONAL FOREST

Zuni Point

The Desert Watchtower, designed
by Mary E. J. Colter, displays
design features from a variety of
southwestern cultures.

Moran Point

p.38
to Grand Canyon Village

LIPAN POINT

Lipan Point provides what might be the best view on the South Rim, and the most informative. Many of the important features of the Canyon story are visible here, along with a broad panorama of regional landmarks (see panorama, page 43).

FLASH FLOODS AND RIVERS OF ROCK

Most of the tributary canyons in the Grand Canyon are dry; where springs supply water, they are often too small to create permanent streams. Yet we say the Canyon was carved by moving water. How is this possible in a dry land? Part of the answer is flash flooding and a strange phenomenon called debris flows. Flash floods happen mostly during summer thunderstorms, although some of the largest on record occurred during unusually heavy rains in December of 1966. Water falling on the desert's bare ground runs off quickly, gathering in short-lived but powerful torrents, carrying quantities of sand and clay and small stones. Flash floods can rise and disappear in a few short hours.

Debris flows are less common events that occur when clay, sand, gravel and even large boulders, mixed with a small amount of water (as little as 15 per cent) begin moving in a cohesive mass — literally flowing, like a stream but mostly made of solids. Sometimes triggered by landslides, they happen fast and transport boulders weighing many tons for miles at a time in a matter of minutes; the biggest ones go all the way to the Colorado River, where they build and alter whitewater rapids.

TUSAYAN MUSEUM AND RUIN TRAIL

Tusayan Ruin is the remains of a pueblo village that has been partially excavated and stabilized. Rangers conduct interpretive walks at frequent intervals daily throughout much of the year. An attractive museum helps visitors picture life at the canyon over 800 years ago.

Judging from its size, Tusayan was a small village housing about 30 people. We know they farmed corn, beans and squash; that they gathered wild food; that they made lovely pottery; that they were probably the ancestors of the modern Hopi, whose name for them is Hisat Sinom. Anasazi, the term used more commonly, is an English word derived from two Navajo words.

Despite all that archeologists have been able to learn, ruins like these still inspire more questions than answers. Even the names of ruins are the inventions of inquisitive modern people. Tusayan, for example, was what Spanish explorers called the Hopi communities located well east of the Grand Canyon. What the builders of this small ruin called it will never be known. Perhaps they called it simply "home."

THE VIEW FROM LIPAN POINT

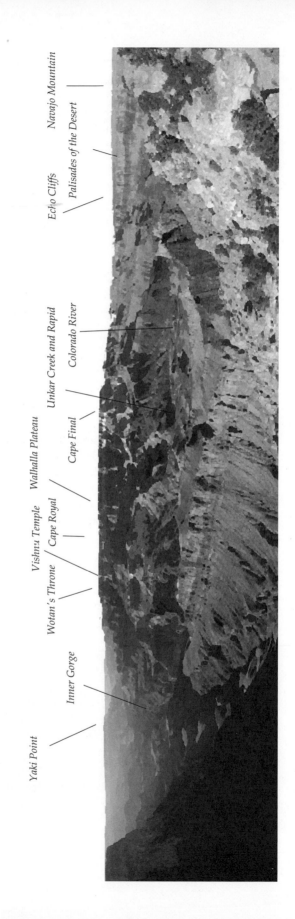

Yaki Point
Inner Gorge
Wotan's Throne
Vishnu Temple
Cape Royal
Walhalla Plateau
Cape Final
Unkar Creek and Rapid
Colorado River
Echo Cliffs
Palisades of the Desert
Navajo Mountain

Panorama From Lipan Point (Elev. 7300')

Although by-passed by many visitors, Lipan Point provides one of the finest panoramas, and perhaps the most instructive view of the Canyon. The Colorado River can be seen making its great turn toward the west. From the Palisades of the Desert, it winds through the relatively soft, red layers of the Grand Canyon Series and then dives into the hard black metamorphics of the Inner Gorge.

The overall structure of the Kaibab Monocline is also clearly evident from here, rising from the flat surface of the Marble Platform (elevation, 6,000 feet) to the heights of the North Rim (8,000 to 9,000 feet); the angles of rock strata reveal the folding that caused the plateau to rise.

The Asymmetrical Canyon

Looking to either side, the southward-slope of the plateau is also evident; its high point lies some miles north of the North Rim. This means that rain falling on the South Rim generally flows away from the Canyon, while water on the North Rim flows into it, causing more erosion on the north side. The result is that the North Rim erodes back away from the river at a faster rate. Cape Royal stands about six horizontal miles from the Colorado, while Lipan Point is only half that distance from the river.

Echo Cliffs

On the eastern horizon, the Echo Cliffs form a barely visible line of red rock. This same rock once overlay the Kaibab Limestone that now forms the Canyon rims; it has eroded back toward the north, standing now like a giant step in what is popularly called the Grand Staircase, a series of ledges and rock layers that climb from the Colorado River to the heights of Zion and Bryce national parks.

Hard Rock, Soft Rock

Characteristics of rock influence the Canyon's shape. The red sedimentary layers of the Unkar Creek Delta are soft and easily eroded. Here the river has carved a broad valley, complete with low rounded hills, where about 800 years ago prehistoric farmers grew corn and other crops. Downstream, the river gnaws at much harder metamorphic rock, creating a steep-sided gorge, where the water flows fast and the rapids become more difficult. Of this section of river, John Wesley Powell wrote in his *Exploration of the Colorado River of the West*:

"Down in these grand, gloomy depths we glide, ever listening, for the mad waters keep up their roar; ever watching, ever peering ahead, for the narrow cañon is winding, and the river is closed in so that we can see but a few hundred yards, and what there may be ahead we know not."

GRAND CANYON

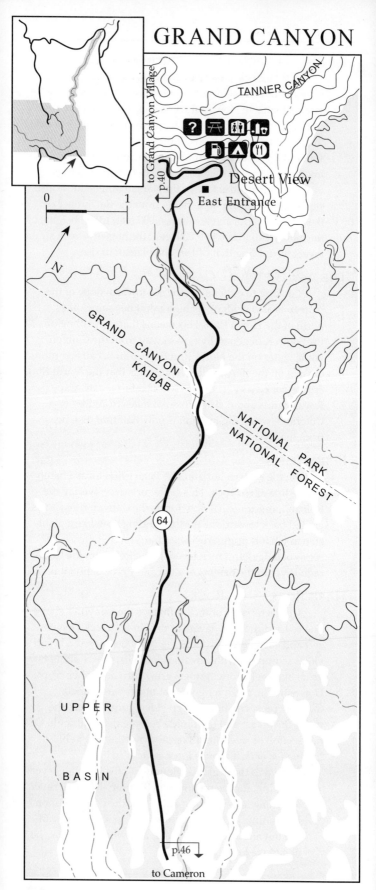

to Grand Canyon Village
p.40

TANNER CANYON

Desert View
East Entrance

GRAND CANYON
KAIBAB

NATIONAL PARK
NATIONAL FOREST

64

UPPER

BASIN

p.46
to Cameron

DESERT VIEW

Desert View is named not for its canyon vistas (which are superb) but for its view to the east, across the Marble Platform toward the Painted Desert. Two distinctly different landscapes are visible from here: The horizontal meets the vertical; flat rock layers of the Marble Platform meet the folded layers of the Kaibab Monocline. This transition is marked by an even more important event: The Colorado River, having made its way south along the edge of the monocline, turns to the west at this point, cutting through the heart of the Kaibab Plateau, a feat of erosion that still challenges geologic explanation.

Services at Desert View include a campground, information center, general store, cafe and souvenir shops; the service station and campground are closed in winter.

DESERT VIEW WATCHTOWER

One of the park's most striking buildings, the Watchtower was designed by architect Mary E. J. Colter and built in the 1930s. Colter took inspiration from similar round structures at Mesa Verde and Canyon de Chelly. The originals, whose real purposes can only be surmised, were built some 800 years ago by the Anasazi (or Hisat Sinom in Hopi terminology). Colter built her tower to a much larger scale (70 feet high, 30 feet in diameter at the base) and incorporated ideas from a variety of Indian cultures. The ground floor curio shop is patterned after a Pueblo kiva, or ceremonial structure. Each level in the tower is decorated in a different style, ranging from modern Hopi art to pictographs in the ancient style. Climbing the tower (by interior stairways) is well worth the small effort.

MARBLE CANYON

North of Desert View, the Colorado River flows through Marble Canyon where, because there has been less faulting and breaking of the rock, the walls are nearly vertical. The canyon takes its name not from true marble but from the smooth, fine-grained limestone into which it has been cut.

EAST ENTRANCE

Admission to Grand Canyon National Park requires a permit, available at this and other entrance stations. See page 10 for a description of fees and types of permits. Also available here are introductory maps and general information, including The Guide, a free park publication with informative articles and a listing of interpretive programs. For more detailed information, stop at the visitor information center at Desert View.

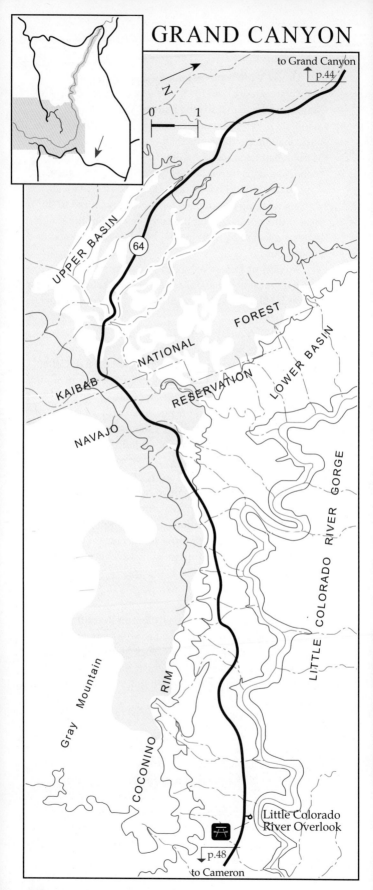

GRAND CANYON

to Grand Canyon
p.44

N

0   1

UPPER BASIN

64

NATIONAL   FOREST

KAIBAB   RESERVATION   LOWER BASIN

NAVAJO

LITTLE COLORADO RIVER GORGE

Gray Mountain

COCONINO RIM

Little Colorado
River Overlook

p.48
to Cameron

THE UPPER BASIN

East of the park, the highway follows an open valley called the Upper Basin, a "step" in the Kaibab Monocline. Over most of its length the monocline forms a single, steep-sided rampart but here it rises on two levels, probably caused by double faulting in rock layers far below the surface. Characteristic of the entire Coconino Plateau, the floor of the Upper Basin shows a distinct dip, or tilt, toward the south away from the Canyon.

Around milepost 278, the road traverses the lower step of the monocline, and crosses the border of the Navajo Reservation. Here are superb views of the startling gorge of the Little Colorado River and country far to the north—mesas and buttes rising above the nearly flat Marble Platform, all the way to cliffs above Lees Ferry, where the Grand Canyon begins.

CEDAR MOUNTAIN

The closest flat-topped mesa is called Cedar Mountain, after the cedar-like juniper trees that cover it. Bearing fossils and petrified wood, the red Moenkopi Sandstone is a remnant of layers that once covered the region, as it still does to the north and east, notably in Zion and Petrified Forest national parks.

KAIBAB MONOCLINE

This is no mere hill standing to the south; it is the Kaibab Monocline, a sharp fold in the earth's surface that has much to do with explaining the Grand Canyon's existence. The earth warped upward here, creating a 3,000-foot high escarpment stretching about 150 miles from the San Francisco Peaks to southern Utah.

At this section of the monocline, called Gray Mountain, rock layers at the top lie flat, as they do over much of the surrounding region. In contrast, steeply tilted slabs on the facing slope show how the rock layers bent and folded as the plateau was forced upward.

LITTLE COLORADO RIVER OVERLOOK

Near milepost 286, a short side road leads to a fine overlook of the Little Colorado Canyon. The "Little C," as locals call this river, begins in northwestern New Mexico, flowing intermittently across open desert. The canyon is 1200 feet deep at this point, while only a few miles east, at Cameron, its walls are low enough that trucks too heavy for the highway bridge can drive across it when water is not flowing. Note that across the canyon stands Shadow Mountain, a black volcanic cone. Here it stands out as an unusual feature, although near Flagstaff there are many such cones.

GRAND CANYON

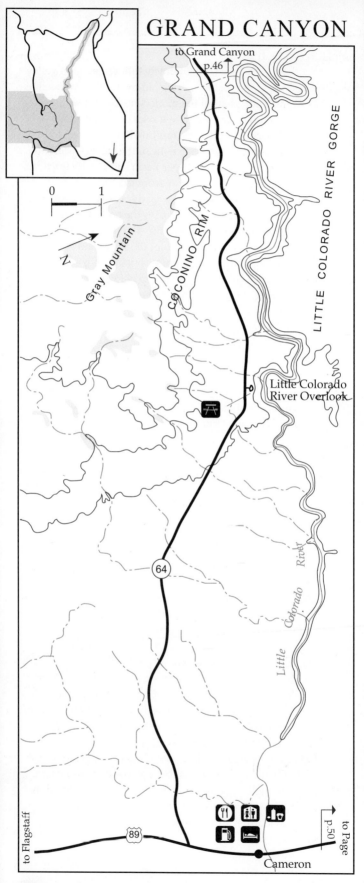

to Grand Canyon
p.46

LITTLE COLORADO RIVER GORGE

Gray Mountain

0   1

N

COCONINO RIM

Little Colorado
River Overlook

64

Little Colorado River

to Page
p.50

89

to Flagstaff

Cameron

DESERT VEGETATION

Near milepost 290, where the Kaibab Monocline turns south, the folding of the rock layers is clearly evident. The road here is about 3,000 feet lower than the South Rim, and 4,000 feet below the North Rim. Instead of forest, blackbrush covers the ground, as it does on the Tonto Platform deep in the Grand Canyon. Wildflowers grow thick along the highway in an interesting example of a human-caused microclimate. Water from infrequent storms collects in the borrow ditches, and the pavement helps keep the ground beneath the road from drying out, so that flowers bloom as if along a creekbed.

POWERLINES

Powerlines march south from the Glen Canyon Dam, carrying electricity to southwestern cities. Completed in 1963 and located 12 river miles above the start of the Grand Canyon, the dam has had a profound impact on the ecology of the Colorado River, controlling river flow and turning the water clear and cold all year. Lacking sediment, the river erodes beaches and cannot build them back up. Because annual floods are controlled, vegetation along riverbanks has been altered. Fish species are different. Recently, extensive scientific studies have been conducted in an attempt to understand fully the changes wrought by this most controversial of dams.

CAMERON

In 1916 Hubert Richardson built the trading post here beside a new suspension bridge, and named the spot for Senator Ralph Cameron who was instrumental in getting the bridge built. In its time the only suspension bridge in Arizona, and although it no longer carries traffic, it still stands beside the modern bridge. Richardson operated the trading post until he retired in 1966.

It is worth stopping just to see the old buildings made of red Moenkopi Sandstone and shaded by big cottonwood and mulberry trees. Behind the motel is a walled garden complete with fountains and artificial brooks; a lovely place, it must have been a particularly amazing sight in the early years.

The trading post now offers a large selection of Indian items like Navajo rugs, Hopi Kachina dolls, silver-and-turquoise jewelry, and so forth; yet it still functions as a traditional trading post, selling all sorts of things used by rural Navajos—hardware, saddles, tack, kerosene lanterns, horseshoes, jugs for drinking water, sheep shears, sheep branding liquid, and various dyes for wool, although the best Navajo weavers continue to use only natural dyes from native desert plants.

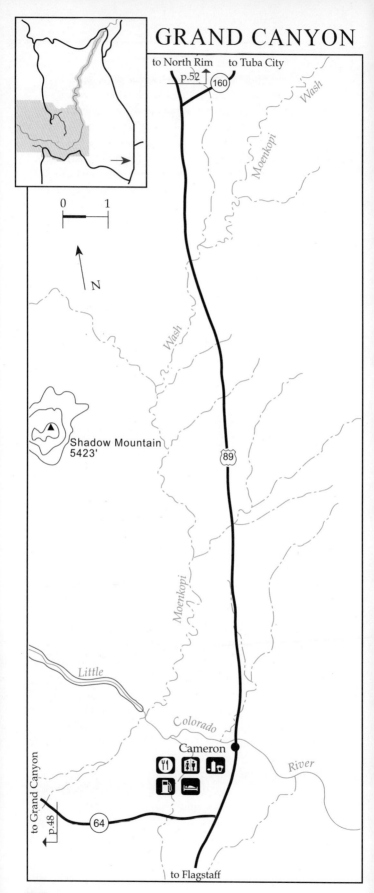

GRAND CANYON

to North Rim   to Tuba City

p.52

160

Wash

Moenkopi

89

Wash

Shadow Mountain
5423'

N

0   1

Moenkopi

Little

Colorado

Cameron

River

to Grand Canyon

p.48

64

to Flagstaff

50

Painted Desert

Colored shale hills to the east of the highway represent a small sample of the Painted Desert, which covers large areas to the east of Flagstaff around Petrified Forest National Park. The name, quite obviously, comes from the natural colors of the rock. Blue, gray, yellow, red, purple, brown and pale green are especially vivid at sunrise or sunset.

Desert Pavement

Around milepost 478 is a good example of desert pavement. Dark pebbles covering the ground are erosion remnants from a layer of Shinarump conglomerate that once overlay the area. Now the loose pebbles, cut loose from their matrix, form a thin but hard surface on the soft shale.

Chinle Hills

The highway rolls through smooth hills of Chinle Shale, made of fine-grained clay and bentonite, a combination that makes an easily eroded, unstable road surface and a strangely appealing landscape. Dust devils, looking like mini-tornadoes, commonly whirl across the open desert in the heat of summer. They are generally harmless, but annoying if you unexpectedly happen to set up your picnic in the path of one.

Last of the Plainsmen

In his book, *The Last of the Plainsmen*, Zane Grey describes a trip by horseback along this route. His party experienced heat, sandstorms, boredom and thirst, but he was nonetheless struck by the desert's beauty: "Thin, clear, sweet, dry, the desert air carried a languor, a dreaminess, tidings of far-off things, and an enthralling promise. The fragrance of flowers, the beauty and grace of women, the sweetness of music, the mystery of life—all seemed to float on that promise. It was the air breathed by the lotus-eaters, when they dreamed, and wandered no more."

Early days at the Cameron Trading Post

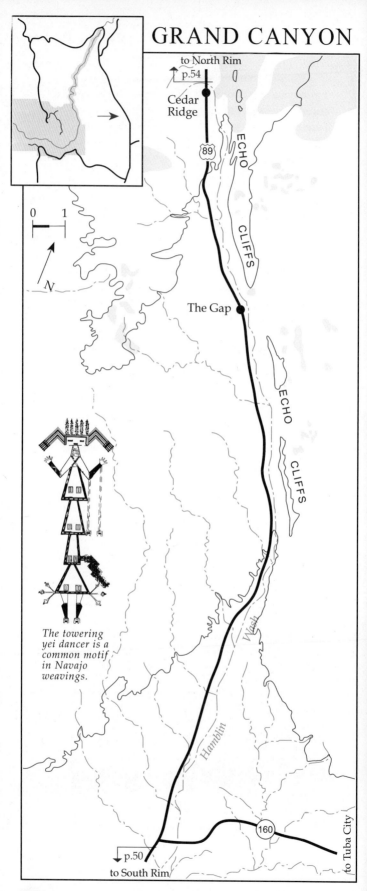

GRAND CANYON

to North Rim
p.54

Cedar
Ridge

89

ECHO CLIFFS

The Gap

ECHO CLIFFS

*The towering
yei dancer is a
common motif
in Navajo
weavings.*

0   1

N

Wash

Hamblin

160

p.50
to South Rim

to Tuba City

Juniper Trees

Vegetation can indicate conditions of moisture and temperature which would otherwise be hard to detect. Near the head of Hamblin Wash, junipers reveal that growing conditions are marginally better than areas just a few miles away. Being higher, it's probably a little cooler and wetter here. The poplars and Russian olives and other broadleafed trees are not native to this place.

Hamblin Wash

Jacob Hamblin was a Mormon explorer, missionary and diplomat who pioneered the route used by Mormon colonists who established towns along the Little Colorado River in east-central Arizona. From near Flagstaff all the way to Jacob Lake and beyond, Hamblin's old road is paralleled by US Highway 89. Although he formalized the route, he was by no means its discoverer. It is a natural path through difficult country, and no doubt has been used for hundreds and maybe thousands of years by assorted residents and travelers.

The Gap

A break, or gap, in the Echo Cliffs marks the site of a trading post. Gravels found here indicate that the San Juan River might have flowed this way long ago. Now the Gap channels powerlines and a rough dirt road that leads eventually to the town of Page.

Echo Cliffs

As the Painted Desert fades away (or begins, depending on one's direction of travel), this imposing line of cliffs rises. The name comes from an incident in 1871, on Powell's second Colorado River expedition. As they emerged from Glen Canyon just upstream from the Paria River, a group of men climbed to a high point above their camp. One of the men, Frederick Dellenbaugh, tried to hit the river with a revolver shot. The river suffered no injury but, after 24 seconds of silence, the report of his shot came echoing back to him, ricocheting among the cliffs. They called the high point Echo Peaks, a name which now applies to this sixty-mile line of cliffs.

Green shrubs and trees mark a series of springs with names that include Hidden, Government, Willow and others. Water has been a major factor in determining settlement patterns in the southwest; here, extra moisture supports a scattering of tamarisk, a thirsty tree more commonly found on riverbanks. Tamarisk is not native to North America. It was imported early in the century as a measure to stabilize riverbanks, but it did more. It took over, quickly spreading to riparian areas across the southwest. In places today it is considered a pest, but nesting birds find it good and there's no denying the beauty and fragrance of its purple flowers.

GRAND CANYON

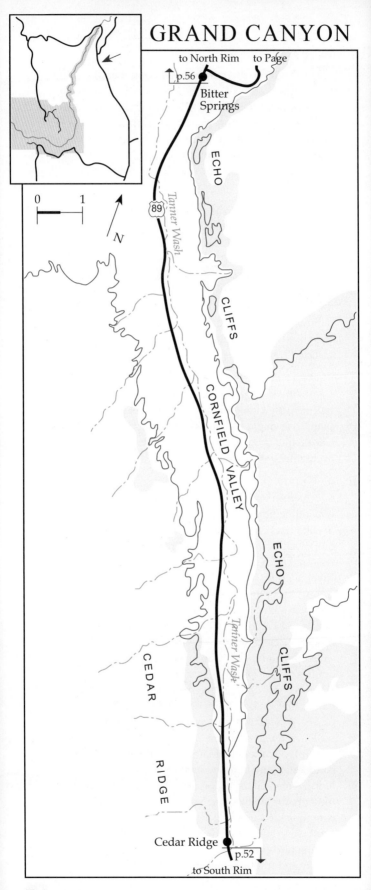

to North Rim   to Page

p.56

Bitter
Springs

ECHO

89

Tanner Wash

CLIFFS

CORNFIELD VALLEY

ECHO

CEDAR

Tanner Wash

CLIFFS

RIDGE

Cedar Ridge

p.52

to South Rim

0   1

N

CORNFIELD VALLEY

Rising beside Tanner Wash, the Echo Cliffs achieve their full height, capped by a distinctive layer of light colored Navajo Sandstone, one of the most recognizable rock layers in the region. The Navajo was laid down not by water, but by wind, originating as great sand dunes in a Sahara-like desert. Averaging some 800 feet thick, and with few impurities or faults to cause zones of weakness, it forms monolithic walls, overhanging alcoves, slot canyons, and smooth horizontal expanses covering the ground like warped pavement. The monuments of Zion National Park and the white domes of Capital Reef National Park are made of Navajo Sandstone. Glen Canyon, now filled by Lake Powell, was a spectacular example of the shapes this sandstone could acquire; some of its side canyons still reveal the unusual water– and wind–carved beauty of this stone.

VERMILION CLIFFS

Travelers headed north get their first good view of the Vermilion Cliffs around milepost 516. They are actually the same geologic formation as the Echo Cliffs, only on the other side of the Colorado River.

HOGANS

Here on the Navajo Reservation, the hogan (pronounced ho-GAHN) is the traditional dwelling. Many Navajo families now live in modern homes but a hogan is usually part of the family compound. Circular (or six-sided), the old-style hogan is built of juniper logs and covered with the native earth. The door always faces east, in honor of the rising sun. Cool in summer, warm in winter, hogans are comfortable structures well-suited to their desert environment.

KAIBAB LIMESTONE

With all the ups and downs on the highway between the North and South rims of the Grand Canyon, it is remarkable that for most of the distance the road travels on the same rock layer — the Kaibab Limestone. Resistant to erosion, it forms a natural cap rock, although lifted and folded and varying over 4,000 feet in elevation between here and the heights of the Kaibab Plateau.

The Arizona gopher snake is a constrictor that feeds mostly on rodents. It can be mistaken for a rattlesnake, but it has no poison and is considered by people of the southwest as a beneficial creature — even an auspicious one.

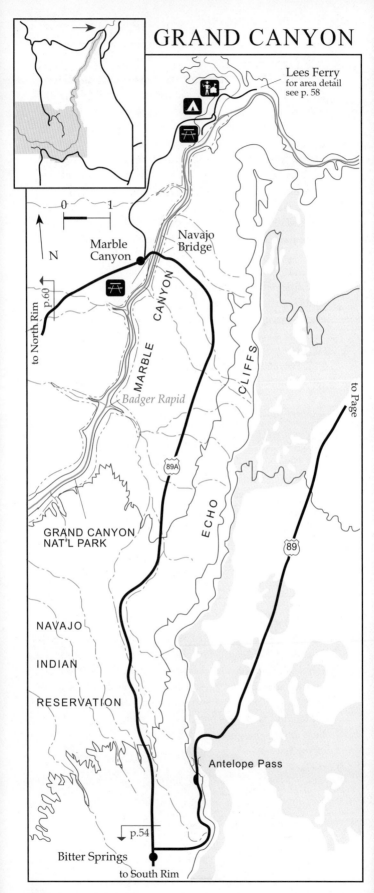

GRAND CANYON

Lees Ferry
for area detail
see p. 58

Navajo
Bridge

Marble
Canyon

p.60

to North Rim

MARBLE CANYON

Badger Rapid

89A

ECHO CLIFFS

to Page

89

GRAND CANYON
NAT'L PARK

NAVAJO

INDIAN

RESERVATION

Antelope Pass

p.54

Bitter Springs

to South Rim

0   1

N

Navajo Bridge Over Marble Canyon

Spanning Marble Canyon at a height of 467 feet above the river, the 834-foot Navajo Bridge replaced Lees Ferry in 1928 as the only Colorado River crossing in the region. Ironically, while the bridge was nearing completion the old ferry capsized and sank, and was never rebuilt.

The river marks the border of the Navajo Reservation. A marble plaque erected in 1961, conspicuously not on the Navajo side, commemorates John Doyle Lee and the wooden ferry "which made possible the colonization of Arizona."

Honeymoon Trail

The highway follows a route dubbed by Mormon settlers the "Honeymoon Trail." In pioneer times Mormon couples, although married in their home towns to the south, had to travel hundreds of miles to St. George, Utah, for officially-sanctioned temple weddings. The trail took them across Lees Ferry, over the Kaibab Plateau at Jacob Lake, and on to St. George via Kanab.

Whitewater in the Canyon

The road passes inconsequential-looking ravines which except during flash floods are dry and silent. At river level, however, hidden at the bottom of Marble Canyon, these ravines and similar ones across the canyon have built the first rapids faced by boaters beginning the 227-mile trip down the Colorado River through the Grand Canyon. The names of these first rapids are Badger, Soap Creek, and House Rock. While not the hardest in the Canyon they are the first, and therefore rank among the most memorable.

Highway 89

The highway to Page, Arizona, climbs along a fault to the top of the Echo Cliffs. Near the rim of the cliffs is a pullout affording a tremendous view of Marble Platform and Marble Gorge. It is worth a short side trip if time allows.

The wooden ferry boat, carrying a wagon and passengers.

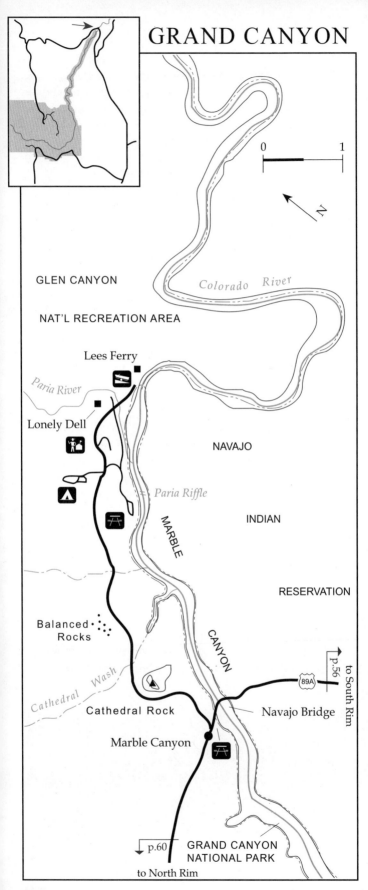

GRAND CANYON

0   1

N

GLEN CANYON

NAT'L RECREATION AREA

Colorado River

Lees Ferry

Paria River

Lonely Dell

NAVAJO

Paria Riffle

MARBLE

INDIAN

RESERVATION

Balanced Rocks

CANYON

Cathedral Wash

p.56

89A

to South Rim

Cathedral Rock

Navajo Bridge

Marble Canyon

p.60

GRAND CANYON
NATIONAL PARK

to North Rim

LEES FERRY

A paved road leads six miles to the site of Lees Ferry, now a part of the Glen Canyon National Recreation Area. For many years, this location was the only feasible river crossing in hundreds of miles. With Glen Canyon upstream, and the Grand Canyon below, Lees Ferry was important to anyone traveling between Arizona and Utah. Today, it provides the only chance for visitors to touch the flowing Colorado River without hiking to the bottom of the Grand Canyon. Facilities include a campground, picnic area, and ranger station. The old ferry buildings and ranch are designated historic districts.

BALANCED BOULDERS

Boulders of Shinarump conglomerate have tumbled from the rim. Coming to rest on the soft Moenkopi formation, they protect the softer rock under them from erosion, until these boulders are left standing on protected pillars. When they fall, as they must eventually, the process will begin anew.

BEGINNING OF THE GRAND CANYON

Here amid upward-slanting rock layers begins the Grand Canyon of the Colorado River. Almost 280 miles downstream, the Grand Wash Cliffs on Lake Mead mark the end of the Canyon. This is the starting point for whitewater boating expeditions; the first take-out point lies 227 wild river miles away at Diamond Creek.

For people eager to get a feel for the river, shorter one-day float trips operate between Glen Canyon Dam and Lees Ferry, originating from Page, Arizona. Also, fishermen go upriver from here in motorboats, lured by excellent trout fishing.

Lees Ferry is named for John Doyle Lee, a Mormon settler who moved here in 1871, established the ferry and built a farm irrigated by the waters of Paria River. He called the ranch Lonely Dell, and for him it was a sort of exile stemming from his involvement in the Mountain Meadows Massacre. Lee was the only man ever brought to trial for the incident, in which 140 California-bound pioneers were massacred by a force of Mormons resentful of US troops in the area. Lee was eventually arrested, and executed in 1877. His wife Emma continued to run the ferry until the Mormon church bought it from her in 1879.

Today, much has changed. The ferry is gone, no longer necessary after the 1928 construction of the Navajo Bridge. The river, emerging from the Glen Canyon Dam, has lost its muddy color. The buildings and Lee's old farm, unoccupied for many years, have been declared a national historic site. A walking tour pamphlet is available for those interested in touring the historic districts.

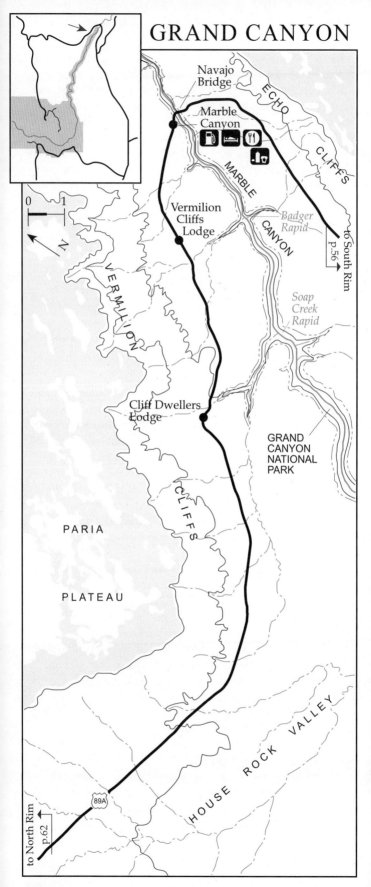

GRAND CANYON

Navajo Bridge

ECHO CLIFFS

Marble Canyon

MARBLE CANYON

Badger Rapid

Vermilion Cliffs Lodge

to South Rim

p.56

Soap Creek Rapid

VERMILION

Cliff Dwellers Lodge

GRAND CANYON NATIONAL PARK

CLIFFS

PARIA

PLATEAU

HOUSE ROCK VALLEY

89A

to North Rim

p.62

0   1

N

VERMILION CLIFFS

For about 30 miles the road travels along the base of the Vermilion Cliffs. The layer that looks like smooth multi-colored clay is Chinle Shale, also visible across the canyon at the base of the Echo Cliffs. The same shale layer forms the strange eroded clay hills 50 miles to the south along Highway 89.

CLIFF DWELLERS LODGE

East of the current lodge buildings are two picturesque stone structures built partly under and around some large balanced boulders. Now unused, they once formed the original Cliff Dwellers Trading Post.

The boulders, having rolled off the cliffs above, stand on uneroded pedestals of soft shale. It seems like a windy day could topple the more precarious of them. Some day they undoubtedly will fall.

HOUSE ROCK VALLEY

Few mountain summits offer better, more expansive views than this open valley. To the east, like a great ocean wave, rises the Kaibab Monocline. About 55 miles south it appears to end abruptly, marking the bend where the Colorado River turns west into the heart of the Grand Canyon and the Kaibab Plateau.

North of the road the Vermilion Cliffs form an imposing line that continues on the other side of Marble Canyon under the name Echo Cliffs. To the south, as if placed intentionally and ceremoniously in the center of all this open space, stands the flat dark mesa called Shin-umo Altar. Marble Canyon itself shows up as a subtle line of shadow in the desert floor. You could walk that way and hardly know the gorge was there until you stepped to its rim, and looked down at the Colorado River, some 1,600 vertical feet below.

The valley was named for two large boulders that form a crude shelter, dubbed Rock House Hotel by an early rancher.

Uncle Jim Owens was an early game warden and hunter who at one time claimed to have shot 532 mountain lions. He joined "Buffalo" Jones in an attempt to cross–breed bison and cattle on the North Rim (see page 63).

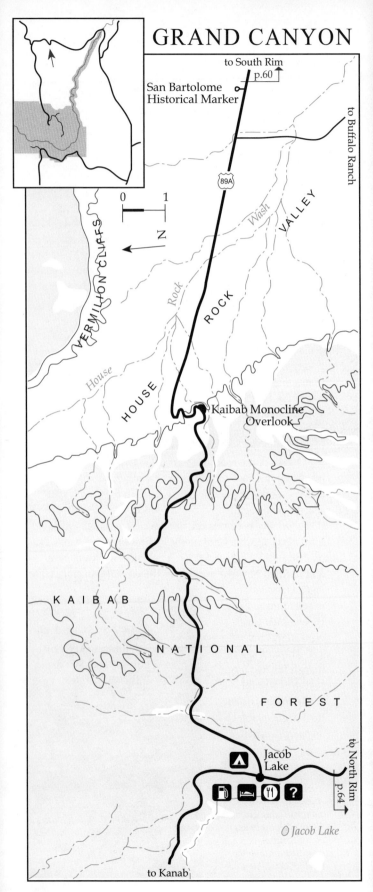

GRAND CANYON

San Bartolome
Historical Marker

to South Rim
p.60

to Buffalo Ranch

89A

ROCK VALLEY

Wash

Rock

VERMILION CLIFFS

House

HOUSE ROCK

Kaibab Monocline
Overlook

K A I B A B

N A T I O N A L

F O R E S T

Jacob
Lake

to North Rim
p.64

○ Jacob Lake

to Kanab

0   1

N

SAN BARTOLOME HISTORICAL MARKER

Plaques give information on several subjects, including the Spanish exploration party which passed this way in late October, 1776, after three months of hard traveling. Led by two Franciscan padres, Silvestre Vélez de Escalante and Francisco Atanasio Domínguez, ten men had set off from Santa Fe looking for an overland route to the Spanish missions in California. In this they failed, stopped by uncertainty and bad weather in central Utah. Working their way homeward, hungry and tired, they came along the base of the Vermilion Cliffs. Fortunately, they had the benefit of advice from local Paiutes, who directed them toward Lees Ferry. Although the river was too high to ford, they kept going upstream and eventually crossed the Colorado in Glen Canyon.

Ignorant of the canyons that lay before them, it must have been hard for that small party to find a way across the river. But it could have been worse. Without local advice they might have headed south, into deeper canyons and greater difficulty.

HOUSE ROCK BUFFALO RANCH

Wild buffalo (or bison) roam this valley on 60,000 acres of national forest land. The animals were brought to Arizona around 1906 by "Buffalo" Jones, a former buffalo hunter and the subject of Zane Grey's book *The Last of the Plainsmen*. About him, Grey wrote: "At last, seeing that the extinction of the noble beasts was inevitable, he smashed his rifle over a wagon wheel and vowed to save the species. For ten years he labored, pursuing, capturing and taming buffalo.... As civilization encroached upon the plains Buffalo Jones ranged slowly westward; and today an isolated desert bound plateau on the north rim of the Grand Canyon of Arizona is his home. There his buffalo browse with the mustang and deer, and are as free as ever they were on the rolling plains."

Not entirely free. Now state property, the herd is kept under 100 animals by controlled hunting. The ranch itself is about 20 miles south (take Forest Road 445; the ranch is open all year, weather permitting).

KAIBAB MONOCLINE OVERLOOK

While driving from one rim of the Canyon to the other, it's an interesting challenge to keep track of major landmarks—to recognize distinctive features from different angles and at great distances. Doing so helps one get a feel for the lay of the land. Few places lend themselves to such long views. Here the road traverses the Kaibab Monocline; 135 highway miles away, it encounters the same geologic feature on the South Rim. Other important features visible throughout the region include the Vermilion Cliffs, Echo Cliffs, Shinumo Altar, and Marble Platform.

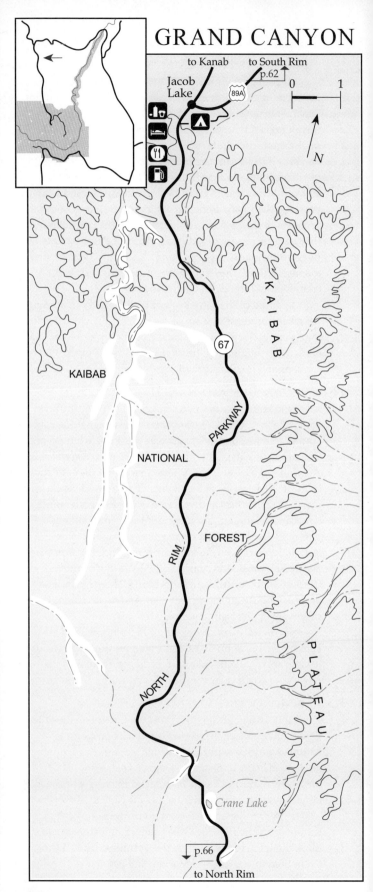

GRAND CANYON

to Kanab

to South Rim
p.62

Jacob
Lake

89A

0   1

N

KAIBAB

KAIBAB

NATIONAL

PARKWAY

FOREST

RIM

PLATEAU

NORTH

Crane Lake

p.66

to North Rim

Jacob Lake

This crossroads offers lodging, fuel, a restaurant, an RV park, a Forest Service campground and the North Kaibab Visitor Center. From the junction, the North Rim Parkway (Arizona Highway 67), provides access to the less crowded side of the Grand Canyon. The road is closed during winter, starting with the first big snowfall, usually in November, until the middle of May.

Although Jacob "Lake" itself is a small sinkhole pond not visible from the highway, it has long been an important place for travelers. Named for the Mormon pioneer Jacob Hamblin, it was one of a few reliable water sources on the long dry trail from central Arizona to Utah — a trail which Hamblin had marked out during explorations in the 1850s and 1860s. It was Hamblin who located the two crossings at either end of the Grand Canyon: Lees Ferry on the upstream end and Pearce Ferry at the Canyon's mouth.

Kaibab Plateau

Aspen trees appear like a message from snowy peaks, and in fact, although no mountains are in sight, the road runs at alpine elevations around 8,000 to 9,000 feet. Thirty miles away on the Marble Platform, lizards skitter through the desert blackbrush. Here, mule deer bound over pine needles in deep forest. Other wildlife includes mountain lions, bobcats, wild turkeys, black bears, coyotes, badgers and numerous smaller animals. Snow lies deep in winter; the average snowfall at the North Rim is around 12 feet per year.

Kaibab comes from two Paiute words, *kaiuw* (mountain) and *a-vwi* (lying down). This "mountain lying down" was a summer home for Paiutes and a trading center for them and other southwestern tribes including the Navajo. The first white settlers called it Buckskin Mountain, reflecting its importance as a source of deer hides.

Crane Lake

The road enters an open meadow and skirts the edge of a tiny lake — more accurately a pond caused by a sinkhole in the underlying limestone. The lakes, evaporating by autumn or freezing up during the long winter, provide a short growing season for aquatic plants and animals.

One species, the Utah Tiger Salamander, adapts to these conditions in an unusual way. Although larvae are common (they resemble large tadpoles), adults are almost never found. This suggests that reproduction might occur through neotony, a biologist's term for sexual maturity in an immature, larval body.

Groups of mule deer emerge from the forest at dawn and dusk to feed on meadow plants, their favorite being three-leafed mountain clover; they eat very little grass.

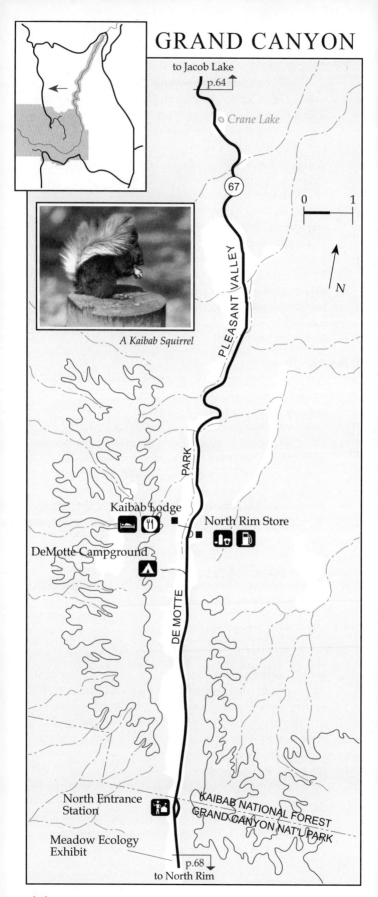

GRAND CANYON

to Jacob Lake

p.64

Crane Lake

67

PLEASANT VALLEY

0   1

N

A Kaibab Squirrel

PARK

Kaibab Lodge

North Rim Store

DeMotte Campground

DE MOTTE

North Entrance
Station

KAIBAB NATIONAL FOREST

GRAND CANYON NAT'L PARK

Meadow Ecology
Exhibit

p.68

to North Rim

DeMotte Park

Services here include the North Rim Country Store, Kaibab Lodge and DeMotte (Forest Service) Campground.

North Entrance Station

From here to the east entrance station on the South Rim is 204 miles by road, compared with a straight line distance of only 18 miles. Birds, obviously, enjoy the best means of travel in canyon country.

Meadow Ecology Display

The road passes through a chain of open meadows called mountain grassland parks. These natural clearings present an interesting puzzle: Why are they here, in the middle of dense forest? Occurring in level basins or valley bottoms, they appear to be self-maintaining, which means they are not temporary clearings created by forest fires or some other outside force. They exist because local conditions discourage trees.

In places, the meadows are ringed by small conifers that seem to be encroaching into the open space, but growth rings show that, although only five feet tall, these trees are as much as thirty years old. For some reason, they are stunted. A few feet away, in the forest proper, trees of the same age are over thirty feet tall.

Why is this? What keeps these meadows open? Theories are many. Perhaps because melted snow and rain collect here, the ground is too wet for tree seeds to germinate. Or maybe toxic gases emitted by soil bacteria inhibit woody plants but not grasses. Or the summer sun might dry seeds so they cannot sprout. But then, how are the stunted trees to be explained?

Kaibab Squirrels

Despite a relative lack of forest, Arizona has more tree squirrel species than any other state. The most famous is arguably the Kaibab squirrel, a conspicuous resident of the North Rim area. A big grey squirrel with white tail and white ear tufts, it can weigh nearly two pounds, averaging 23 ounces. Females are normally a bit heavier than males. They are close relatives of Abert squirrels, which live on the South Rim and in the forests of central Arizona. The Abert, however, lacks the distinctive white tail and ears.

Kaibab squirrels depend on the mature ponderosa pine forest for food and shelter. In spring they eat the flowers of the pines; in summer, seeds from the cones. They dig for fungi ("truffles") that grow among the pine roots, supplementing their diet with insects, various seeds and the acorns from Gambel oak. In winter, life is more difficult. When snow covers the ground, squirrels gnaw the inner bark of pine twigs, a poor food that will not sustain them for long periods.

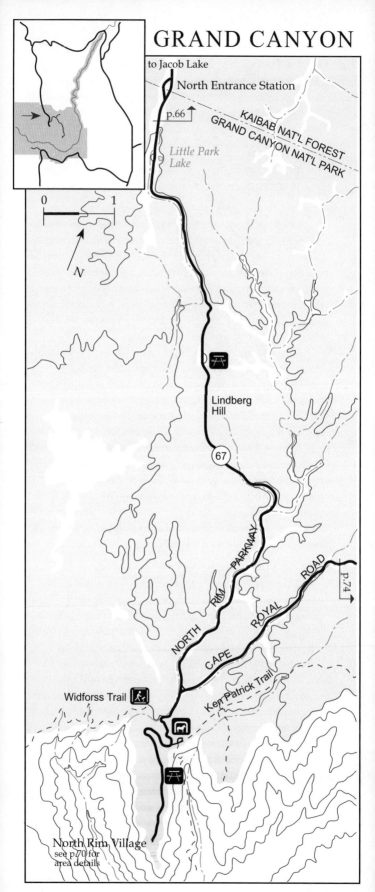

GRAND CANYON

to Jacob Lake

North Entrance Station

p.66

KAIBAB NAT'L FOREST

GRAND CANYON NAT'L PARK

Little Park
Lake

0   1

N

Lindberg
Hill

67

NORTH RIM PARKWAY

CAPE ROYAL ROAD

p.74

Widforss Trail

Ken Patrick Trail

North Rim Village
see p70 for
area details

KAIBAB DEER HERD

The story of the Kaibab deer became a classic biologic cautionary tale. As the story goes, establishment of the Grand Canyon Game Preserve in 1906 protected deer and encouraged killing of predators; and as a result, the deer herd went from 4,000 animals to 100,000 by 1924. Subsequent overgrazing and two hard winters caused starvation, and the population fell to less than 10,000 deer on a damaged range.

This event has been cited as a clear example of predator-prey relationships. However, as in all natural systems, the story is complicated by other factors. As many as 200,000 sheep and thousands of cattle were also removed after 1906; the habitat had been altered by grazing and fire; and there might never have been 100,000 deer at all. Few details are clear, and in the end, the "classic" story teaches a different lesson—that natural events are usually more complex than they might first appear.

CAPE ROYAL ROAD

This road leads to a series of overlooks, including Point Imperial (8 miles) and Cape Royal (23 miles). Allow at least half a day. Details begin on page 75.

WIDFORSS TRAIL

A gravel road leads about half a mile to a parking area and the Widforss Trailhead. The trail is five miles each way, following the rim of Transept Canyon to Widforss Point. The first 2½ miles are a self–guided nature trail that rambles through a mixed forest of pine, aspen, spruce and fir. Trail booklets are available at the trailhead. The trail is moderate, the views are good, and the setting is peaceful. As with any Canyon trail, be sure to carry water.

Gunnar Mauritz Widforss was a Swedish painter who fell in love with the American West, particularly the national parks. He lived at the Grand Canyon for a number of years and was buried at the South Rim after his death in 1934.

NORTH KAIBAB TRAILHEAD

The most popular trail into the canyon from the North Rim, the North Kaibab was a faint Indian trail when mapping crews began using it in the early 1900s. In those years, North Rim guides Dave Rust and Uncle Jim Owens used the trail to take tourists to the river and back. Rust built a camp at the mouth of Bright Angel Creek in 1905; it later became Phantom Ranch. With only sporadic maintenance, the route remained difficult until the Park Service completed the cross-canyon trail, the Kaibab, in 1928. In its 14.2 miles, the North Kaibab descends from about 8,200 to 2,400 feet in elevation. Strong day hikers can make the trek down to Roaring Springs and back, 4.7 miles and 3,200 vertical feet each way.

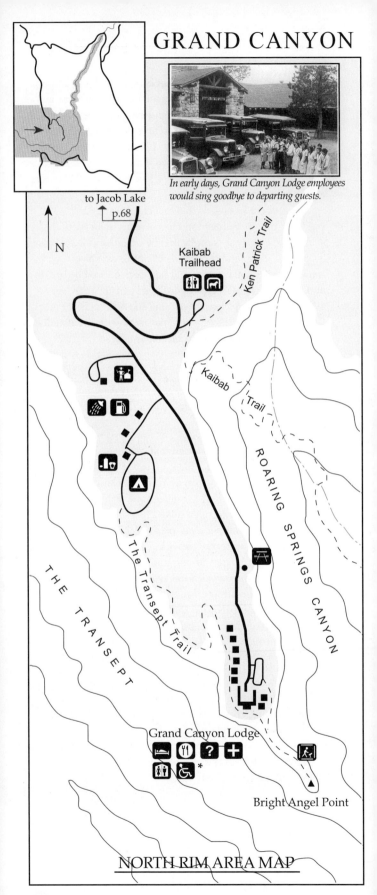

GRAND CANYON

In early days, Grand Canyon Lodge employees would sing goodbye to departing guests.

to Jacob Lake
p.68

N

Kaibab Trailhead

Ken Patrick Trail

Kaibab Trail

ROARING SPRINGS CANYON

The Transept Trail

THE TRANSEPT

Grand Canyon Lodge

Bright Angel Point

NORTH RIM AREA MAP

North Rim

Approaching the North Rim can be a bit confusing. The road ends not at a stunning viewpoint, but in the courtyard of the Grand Canyon Lodge. To see the Canyon, park just before the lodge and walk either to Bright Angel Point (bear left around the buildings) or through the lobby of the lodge to its stone-walled terraces.

Services

Lodging, restaurants, campground, laundromat, showers, a clinic staffed by a Nurse Practitioner, Park Service offices, and other facilities are here. The season runs from mid-May to late October, depending on snow conditions. For phone numbers and more information, see pages 12-15.

Bigger Even Than It Looks

From the lodge terrace, only a small section of the Grand Canyon is visible. To get a sense of its real size, consider that the mountains on the western horizon (the Uinkarets, sometimes not visible due to atmospheric haze) are about 60 air miles away. The entire Canyon, from Lees Ferry to Lake Mead, stretches three times that distance.

Distant Mountains

Like jagged teeth on the southern horizon the volcanic San Francisco Peaks rise to over 12,000 feet in elevation, high enough to be snow-capped much of the year. Bill Williams Mountain and various smaller mountains, all the result of volcanism, range along the horizon westward. In the middle distance, Red Butte is a remnant of soft red layers that once overlay the Kaibab Limestone on both sides of the Grand Canyon; those layers, up to 5,000 feet thick, were stripped away by erosion. Visitors coming from Utah will have passed through country where those red layers still exist—around Kanab and points north.

Things To Do At The North Rim

Hiking: No one should miss the short walk to Bright Angel Point. Other walks include: the Transept Trail (1.5 miles), along the rim between the campground and the lodge; the Ken Patrick Trail (10 miles), between Point Imperial and the North Kaibab Trailhead; the Widforss Trail (5 miles each way); and the North Kaibab Trail, which leads all the way to the Colorado River, but even a short walk is worthwhile. **Mule rides:** Riding a mule into the Canyon is a tradition and, for many, the preferred method of travel. Book saddle space at the Grand Canyon Lodge. **Scenic drives:** The Cape Royal Road can occupy a full day of touring. The climax, Cape Royal, provides some of the Canyon's best sunset views. **Ranger programs:** a full schedule of interpretive walks and informal lectures is offered by the Park Service. For a schedule, visit the information desk in the Grand Canyon Lodge.

THE VIEW FROM BRIGHT ANGEL POINT

Labels: Oza Butte, Bright Angel Fault, Indian Garden, Grand Canyon Village, Summer Butte, Red Butte, Zoroaster Temple, Brahma Temple, Deva Temple, San Francisco Peaks, Angel's Gate, Obi Point

BRIGHT ANGEL CANYON

TRANSEPT CANYON

Bright Angel Point (Elev. 8145')

In all the national parks, there are few short trails that rival this one. A quarter mile in length, this paved path follows a knife-edge ridge separating two chasms. It ends on a narrow point of rock overlooking Transept Canyon on the right and Roaring Springs Canyon on the left. Bright Angel Canyon stretches off toward the distant Colorado River. It is an easy trail, but the altitude can make it feel strenuous.

Transept Canyon Rockfall

Across Transept Canyon (on the right) the light-colored scar of a recent rockfall is visible. In January of 1991, a large piece of Coconino Sandstone fell across the sloping red Hermit Shale and continued to the bottom of the canyon. No one was here to witness the crash. Although it may seem to be an eternal, unmoving landscape, the Grand Canyon is in a state of constant change. Erosion continues as it has for millions of years. Softer rocks like shale erode in smaller pieces, grain by grain, undercutting the harder cliffs, which give way in large slabs. It is a slow process when measured against the span of our lives, not to mention our short visits to this place; but in geologic terms, the Grand Canyon is a relatively recent phenomenon.

South Rim

Ten miles away, the Bright Angel Trail can be seen descending in a series of switchbacks from the South Rim to Indian Garden, where springs support a grove of cottonwood trees—bright green in summer, yellow in fall. The trail descends the canyon wall in a cleft caused by the Bright Angel Fault. Notice the displacement of layers; the western (right-hand) side of the fault is 186 feet higher than the eastern side. On this side of the river, Bright Angel Canyon was eroded along the same, straight fault line.

Also on the South Rim, a few miles to the east, another trail can be seen at the bottom of a long reddish ridge: The South Kaibab Trail and Cedar Ridge. This trail, like the Bright Angel Trail, eventually reaches Phantom Ranch at river level (not visible from here).

Roaring Springs Canyon

On the left of the overlook, this canyon takes its name from a generous natural spring. You can hear the water cascading far below, and see a short stretch of the spring-fed stream. Not all the water flows downhill. A pump house built in 1928 lifts water to the North Rim; a second pipeline, finished in 1970, carries another portion across the Canyon to Indian Garden, where a second pumping station forces it up to the South Rim for use there.

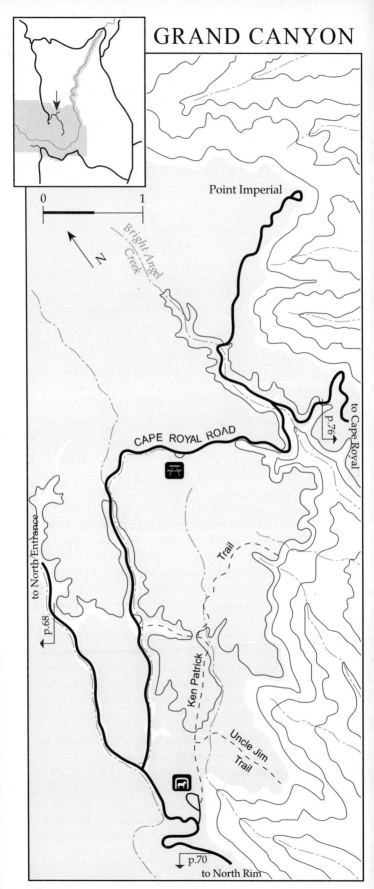

GRAND CANYON

Point Imperial

Bright Angel Creek

CAPE ROYAL ROAD

to Cape Royal

p.76

to North Entrance

p.68

Trail

Ken Patrick

Uncle Jim Trail

p.70

to North Rim

CAPE ROYAL ROAD

This road, 23 miles long, is the major excursion route for autos on the North Rim. Highlights along the way include **Point Imperial** (a good place to watch sunrise), **Vista Encantadora**, **Walhalla Glades Ruin**, a small prehistoric pueblo, and **Angel's Window**, a remarkable rocky viewpoint pierced by a "window" that frames a view of the Colorado River. The road is slow, winding, and often stunningly scenic. Allow at least half a day for this drive.

POINT IMPERIAL (ELEV. 8803')

From Point Imperial, the Grand Canyon seems almost one-sided. Across the Colorado River, where you might expect to see the classic tiered cliffs of the other side of the Canyon, there stretches a great flat expanse — the Marble Platform, nine miles away, averaging about 3,000 feet lower than Point Imperial and seemingly as smooth as a billiard table.

Looking closer, however, you'll notice that the familiar rock layers are in fact still there, just lower. Both here at Point Imperial and on the Marble Platform, the rims consist of Kaibab Limestone. Point Imperial, the highest viewpoint on either rim, achieved its height by riding the Kaibab Monocline as it pushed upward. Looking south, the flexure of rock layers can be clearly seen.

BRIGHT ANGEL CREEK

The road to Point Imperial (turn left at the junction) follows Bright Angel Creek. Here, it is a small forest canyon, almost a ravine. About one mile south, it begins a steep drop, soon becoming the great side canyon visible from Bright Angel Point.

FOREST NOTES

The road winds through dense, sometimes tangled forest of mixed conifers and aspen trees. Conifer species include Engelmann's spruce, blue spruce, Douglas fir, white fir, and ponderosa pine. This cool montane forest is home to deer, coyotes, porcupines, cougar, red squirrels, wild turkeys, flickers, Stellar's and pinyon jays, and other species, many of which are not found just a few miles away below the Canyon rim or on the surrounding desert lands.

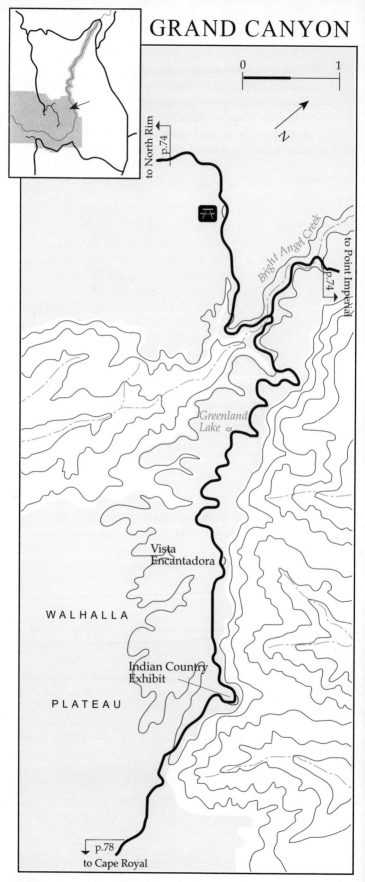

GRAND CANYON

0   1

N

to North Rim
p.74

to Point Imperial
p.74

Bright Angel Creek

Greenland Lake

Vista Encantadora

WALHALLA

Indian Country Exhibit

PLATEAU

p.78
to Cape Royal

WALHALLA PLATEAU

The Walhalla Plateau is a peninsula reaching out, and down, into the Canyon. The road descends gradually along the incline of the Kaibab Plateau, not reaching the South Rim of course, but more closely resembling it in terms of elevation and climate. Notice that aspen and fir and spruce drop away as the plateau gets lower, warmer, and drier.

GREENLAND LAKE

An interpretive display here tells about karst (eroded limestone) topography. Limestone is water soluble, easily dissolved into a complex of underground caves and channels. This explains why, on the North Rim, melting snow and rain drains underground rather than forming surface streams. Depressions and sinkholes are common, and caused by the collapse of underground chambers. They serve as drains unless enough mud and debris collects in them to plug their outlets; in that case, they become ponds like the one here.

Greenland Lake is a natural sinkhole pond enhanced by a man-made check dam left over from pioneer times when cattle grazed this area. As if to demonstrate the unreliability of water on the rim, the "lake" dries up sporadically.

VISTA ENCANTADORA

Because there is such a range of climate and vegetation between the canyon rim and the river, it is often said that being here is like standing in Canada and looking down at southern Arizona. Not quite. The model fails to account for many factors that differ between here and the sub-arctic — for example, winter days are longer at this southerly latitude, solar intensity is stronger because of the high elevation (here about 8,500 feet), and the Canyon rim causes local variations in moisture, sun exposure and temperature. Yet the basic concept is useful. The plants here are indeed more typical of Canada than Arizona. There are no saguaro or cholla cacti, after all. And standing here during a late May snowstorm, it's easy to wonder if Canada is not in fact a warmer place than northern Arizona.

INDIAN COUNTRY

This pullout offers an expansive view across Marble Platform to the Navajo and Hopi reservations. It is a big colorful land where ancient cultures and values survive alongside modern changes. The way of life has been shaped by a spectacular setting that features such places as Monument Valley (location of far too many western movies and television ads), the Painted Desert, Navajo National Monument with its spectacular cliff dwellings, and Petrified Forest National Park.

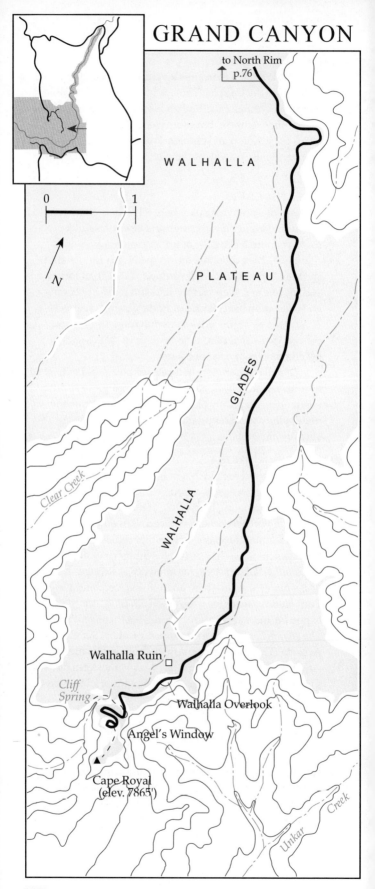

GRAND CANYON

WALHALLA GLADES RUIN

Occupied for about a hundred years between 1050 and 1150 A.D., this small village was probably inhabited by people from the Unkar Delta who came here during the summer to tend crops. A self-guiding brochure is available from a trail-side box; it includes a map of the ruin and interesting details about its excavation.

WALHALLA OVERLOOK

A roadside display gives information about archeological investigations on the Unkar Delta, the open, red-soiled section of Canyon bottom visible to the southeast. The river bends sharply around a fan of erosional debris deposited by Unkar Creek, a fertile location for the Anasazi farmers who lived from around 850 A.D. until almost 1200 A.D. Artifacts and the foundations of the homes which they left behind tell an incomplete but fascinating story of how people lived in the Canyon a thousand years ago.

At first these delta dwellers lived and farmed on terraces close to the river. Later, they moved their houses to rocky slopes on the perimeter of their fields, perhaps because a growing population required that they use all arable land for crops. They also built summer homes near fields on the North Rim; one of these, the Walhalla Glades Ruin, lies just across the road.

ANGEL'S WINDOW

From a curve at the bottom of a short steep hill, this amazing rock comes into sudden view. A small turnout is available for those who wish to stop, although a short distance further is the parking area for Cape Royal; a trail from there leads out on top of the window.

Angel's Window

The trail across the road from this small turnout follows a ravine through the forest to Cliff Spring (one mile round trip). On the way is a small Indian ruin with a good example of a prehistoric granary, or storage room.

CAPE ROYAL

The large parking lot is an indication of this overlook's popularity. Many hours can be spent strolling or sitting along the rim here, watching the light change on the rock formations, or trying to make sense of the enormous geography spread out at one's feet. The trail is marked by interpretive signs telling about plants and animals in the pinyon-juniper woodland. The foot path leads first to Angel's Window, then proceeds to Cape Royal itself.

SUNSET CRATER AND WUPATKI NATIONAL MONUMENTS

A 36-mile paved loop road leads to two national monuments. One tells a story of spectacular volcanic activity, while the other reveals aspects of ancient cultures. Although they might seem to be quite distinct, the two sites have an intertwined history.

Sunset Crater National Monument preserves a classic 1000-foot high volcanic cone and an impressive lava flow at its base. In 1064, the year before the Norman conquest of England, Sunset Crater erupted violently, spewing ash and cinders over an 800-square mile area. Intermittent eruptions continued for over a century after that, dramatically altering the landscape. In its last activity, the crater ejected cinders rich in iron and sulphur, that when oxidized formed the reddish sunset-colored rim from which the crater takes its name. Although quiet now, and not expected to erupt again in the near future, parts of the landscape look as if they were hot just yesterday. Rarely can one stand on such new-born geology as this.

Wupatki National Monument is a 56-square mile archeological site, once the home of several different cultural groups who came together on this site for about two centuries. Following the eruption of Sunset Crater Volcano, the ancient people moved into the Wupatki Basin vicinity. The volcanic ash may have helped the soil to retain the scant moisture and thus create improved conditions for crops. The climate might also have been marginally wetter in those years. During the 1100s, the population hit a peak of perhaps 2,000 people but for reasons not fully understood, they were all gone from the Wupatki area by around 1225.

Today, thousands of abandoned structures, some well preserved, dot the landscape. These are not the impressive

CINDER HILLS AND AA LAVA

The road follows the base of Sunset Crater along the edge of the Bonito Lava Flow, where the soft contours of cinder hills contrast sharply with the jagged aa lava. That plants grow at all on such ground is surprising, yet many species thrive here. In June or July, pink penstemon blooms seem to carpet the cinder hills; please don't pick them.

CINDER HILLS OVERLOOK

This point provides a view of the northeast side of Sunset Crater, and the surrounding cinder hills. Although all the hills are volcanic, and ejected their own cinders and lava at some point in the past, most of the black cinders that cover them now are from Sunset Crater, whose ashes were blown by the wind in a northeast direction. Conspicuous in all the black is a line of red cinder mounds that mark a fissure beneath the surface. The red mounds were formed during the most recent activity of this volcanic field.

VOLCANOES

Over 400 cinder cones and volcanic mountains occur in the area, all part of the San Francisco volcanic field, which over a period of several million years spewed lava across some 2,000 square miles. Considering that long period of activity, it is reasonable to wonder if Sunset Crater was the end of it. Is there more coming? A partial answer to this question was provided by the US Geological Survey after the eruption of Mount St. Helens, which lasted from 1980 to 1983. A list was prepared, ranking the nation's volcanic areas for active potential. This volcanic field ranks low on that list and is expected to remain quiet for the foreseeable future. Still at the top of the list is Mount St. Helens, followed by other west coast mountains.

PONDEROSA PINES

The forest is dominated by ponderosa pines—tall, long-needled trees with reddish scaly bark. Travelers coming from Flagstaff, or from either rim of the Grand Canyon, will notice that the forest here is relatively sparse. Because water drains quickly through these porous cinders, the trees have developed wide, shallow root systems to capture as much water as possible.

PAINTED DESERT VISTA

At an elevation just above 6000 feet, this viewpoint stands near the upper edge of the pinyon-juniper forest, which itself disappears in the lower, warmer and drier distance—first the pinyons, then the junipers. A picnic area offers shaded tables and, most of the year, Stellar's jays give you their opinions on any subject that comes to mind.

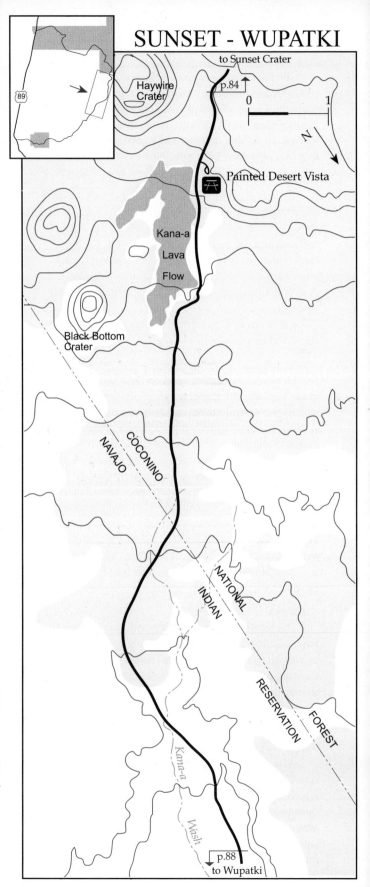

SUNSET - WUPATKI

to Sunset Crater

p.84

0   1

N

Haywire Crater

Painted Desert Vista

Kana-a Lava Flow

Black Bottom Crater

NAVAJO

COCONINO

NATIONAL

INDIAN

RESERVATION

FOREST

Kana-a

Wash

p.88

to Wupatki

LIVING IN THE DESERT

The road skirts the south edge of the Strawberry Crater Wilderness. In the desert scrub, coyotes hunt jackrabbits among the fourwing saltbush and Mormon tea shrubs. Short-horned lizards, commonly known as horned toads, wander like miniature dinosaurs eating ants, their primary food.

This is dry country, averaging only seven to nine inches of rainfall per year, half of what falls just a few miles away at Sunset Crater. Yet for the plants and animals that live here, it is exactly the right amount of water. They are so well adapted to arid conditions that if the climate were to become wetter, many of these creatures would disappear. In that sense, aridity can be as important as moisture in determining what lives where.

Some desert animals can survive without ever taking a drink. They get sufficient water from the food they eat, which always contains a little moisture, and conserve it through a variety of physical and behavioral adaptations. For example, desert animals avoid the heat of day by going underground or staying in the shade. The big ears of jackrabbits, dense with blood vessels, serve as cooling organs and substitute for sweating or panting.

The champions of water conservation belong to a family of rodents called *Heteromyids,* including the pocket mouse and the kangaroo rat, who can survive indefinitely on metabolic water—that is, moisture resulting from the digestion of food. All animals produce such moisture, but few could survive on such a small amount. These capable little rodents do it by virtue of extra-effective kidneys, the ability to excrete virtually dry droppings, nasal passages that condense water before it leaves the body, and by moving about only at night. The kangaroo rat moves like its namesake, leaping on its hind legs, sometimes seen hopping across the road in the beam of headlights.

THE WITHOUT-WATER PEOPLE

The prehistoric people who lived here and built such structures as Wukoki had also to adapt to desert conditions, a fact reflected by archeologists' name for them: Sinagua, which is Spanish for "without water" and which also once referred to the San Francisco Peaks. The names are appropriate, as in the whole Wupatki Basin there are few permanent springs. People, like the other creatures, depended on sparse rainfall and conservation techniques.

BLACK ROCK, RED ROCK

At 4800 feet elevation, the red sedimentary layers of Moenkopi Sandstone emerge beneath the black volcanic rocks and cinders from the San Francisco Volcanic Field.

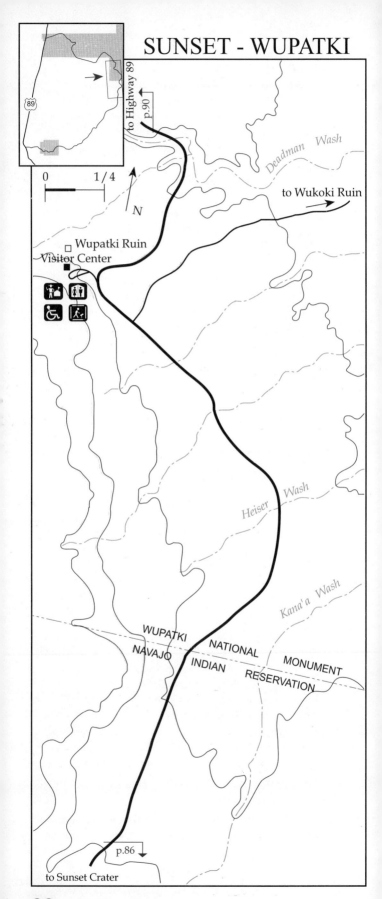

SUNSET - WUPATKI

to Highway 89 p.90

Deadman Wash

to Wukoki Ruin

□ Wupatki Ruin
Visitor Center ■

N

0   1/4

Heiser Wash

Kana'a Wash

WUPATKI

NAVAJO   NATIONAL

INDIAN   MONUMENT

RESERVATION

p.86

to Sunset Crater

WUPATKI RUIN

With almost 100 rooms and in places four stories high, Wupatki was the home of perhaps 125 people of the Sinagua culture. Although deserted for centuries and now far from the beaten path, Wupatki was once a busy place on an important prehistoric trade route. Artifacts found here could only have come from far away: sea-shell jewelry, copper bells, the feathers of parrots, and pottery of non-Sinaguan style. One of Wupatki's outstanding features, the **Ball Court**, is a cultural import—thought to be a playing field for a vigorous ball game similar to that played by the ancient Aztecs and Mayans. Also of interest is a **blowhole**, a vent connected to a large network of underground air space that "breathes" with changes in atmospheric air pressure.

VISITOR CENTER

Located beside Wupatki Ruin, the visitor center offers exhibits which illustrate aspects of prehistoric life in the Wupatki Basin. A full-scale model of a pueblo room gives an idea of living conditions when the village was occupied. The ruin trail begins here.

WUKOKI RUIN

A 2.5-mile side road leads to Wukoki (Hopi for "big house"), a three-story ruin built of Moenkopi Sandstone. It is thought to have been the former home of two or three families from the Sinagua culture, farmers who lived in the area of the San Francisco Peaks for some 500 years until they abandoned their homes around 1225 A.D.

These carefully built stone walls marked an important cultural change for the Sinagua people—a change that occurred after the eruption of Sunset Crater when, having fled from their fields around the active volcano, they discovered that crops would grow in this new area, perhaps as a result of the thin blanket of fresh cinders.

Before that time, the only people in the Wupatki Basin were wandering hunters and gatherers—people whose way of life required that they keep moving in a continual search for game and edible wild plants. If they built houses at all, they were not meant to stand for long, nor were they made of stone. Most likely they were simple brush shelters that have long since vanished from the landscape.

Permanent dwellings developed with agriculture, and the need to stay near one's fields. Sinaguans elsewhere, and prior to the eruption, lived in "pit houses," set partially into the ground and roofed with brush and soil somewhat like traditional Navajo hogans. The people who moved here after the eruption, however, found a ready building material in the Moenkopi Sandstone, and perhaps inspired by the neighboring Anasazi culture, built durable structures like Wukoki.

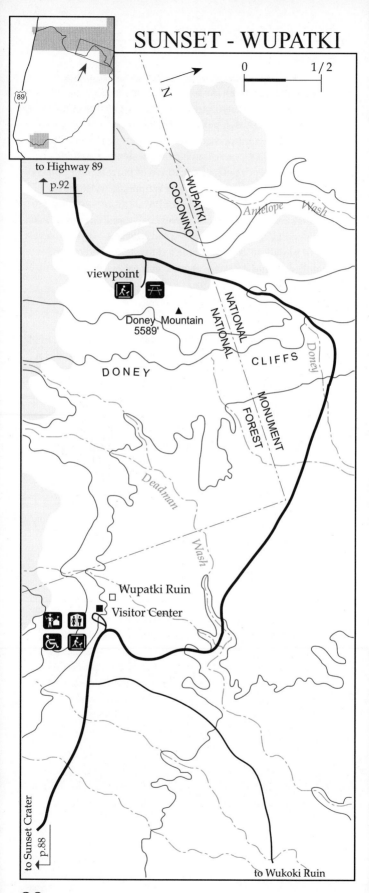

SUNSET - WUPATKI

0   1/2

N

to Highway 89
p.92

WUPATKI COCONINO

Antelope Wash

viewpoint

Doney Mountain
5589'

NATIONAL   NATIONAL

Doney

DONEY   CLIFFS

MONUMENT   FOREST

Deadman

Wash

Wupatki Ruin
Visitor Center

to Sunset Crater
p.88

to Wukoki Ruin

NATURE NOTE

Scattered junipers mark the frontier between forest and grassland. At higher elevations, pinyon pine grow among the junipers to form the southwest's classic "P–J" forest but in the heat and aridity of this lower-altitude zone, junipers prove to be the hardier species. Sometimes called "cedar," the juniper provides many useful products, from firewood to fence posts. Navajos traditionally used its stringy bark for baby diapers, sandals and blankets; they made dye from its berries, gum from its sap, medicine from its leaves and jewelry from its seeds. Some of these uses are still in practice.

DONEY PICNIC AREA AND VIEWPOINT

Here is a fine view eastward framed by two cinder cones; the one on the left is Doney Crater, named for an area pioneer, Ben Doney. Hopi Buttes, some 60 miles away, can be seen on the far horizon, across the Little Colorado River Valley. The eruption of Doney Crater, with its associated cinder cones and lava flows, was the most recent volcanic event in Wupatki, occurring about 15,000

A petroglyph, found in Wupatki, showing geometric patterns similar to those used on ancient ceramics.

years ago (the fine black cinders seen along the road rained down from the more recent Sunset Crater eruptions). A half-mile nature trail leads along the ridge formed by the three smaller craters, affording expansive views from the San Francisco Peaks to Hopi Buttes and the surrounding area.

DONEY MOUNTAIN AND DONEY CLIFFS

The road crosses a fault marking the Black Point monocline. The buff-colored rock is Kaibab Limestone. The red is Moenkopi Sandstone. A casual observer, seeing that the Kaibab forms the cliffs, might think that the Moenkopi lies beneath the Kaibab. In fact, the reverse is true; faulting has shifted the layers, and erosion has stripped the soft red rock from the higher surface but not the lower.

KAIBAB LIMESTONE

The buff-colored surface rock is Kaibab Limestone, the same rock that forms both rims of the Grand Canyon. Folded, faulted, warped and lifted to various elevations, stripped of the softer rocks that once covered it, this erosion-resistant layer soon becomes familiar to observant travelers in Grand Canyon country.

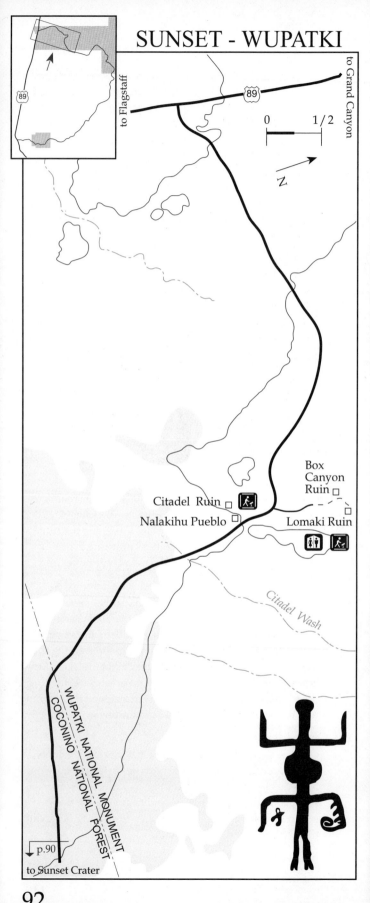

SUNSET - WUPATKI

89
to Flagstaff
to Grand Canyon

0   1/2

Z

Box
Canyon
Ruin

Citadel Ruin

Nalakihu Pueblo

Lomaki Ruin

Citadel Wash

WUPATKI NATIONAL MONUMENT
COCONINO NATIONAL FOREST

p.90
to Sunset Crater

92

BOX CANYON AND LOMAKI RUIN

A half-mile road leads to these two ruins, both located on the edge of earthcracks, or fissures in the underlying limestone caused by volcanic activity.

Lomaki is a modern Hopi word meaning "beautiful house," an appropriate name for a dwelling in such a scenic place. Home to perhaps several families, it was inhabited for about a century.

Although the climate 800 years ago was not much different from today's climate, the landscape has changed with time. When Lomaki was inhabited, the people gathered wood, hunted animals, grew crops, and collected wild edible plants. This no doubt had an impact on their surroundings, as did the modern grazing of cattle, a practice that ended only in 1989 when the monument was finally fenced off from open range. Yet the biggest change is the most dramatic. At least for part of the time when people lived here, Sunset Crater was an active volcano. Standing beside Lomaki on a quiet evening, watching sunset ignite the clouds above the San Francisco Peaks, it is possible to imagine how different it would feel to be here when clouds of ash billowed above the cinder hills of a landscape in the process of creation.

Note the check dam built in the bottom of the earth crack just below the house, another sign of the efforts needed to conserve water in a dry land.

CITADEL RUIN AND NALAKIHU PUEBLO

Citadel Ruin, an unexcavated, fortress-like structure, rules a commanding view from atop a lava mesa, the lava being a remnant from a flow that occurred some one to two million years ago. **Nalakihu Pueblo** stands at the base of the Citadel. Of course archeologists have no idea what the residents of these structures called their homes. Nalakihu is a modern Hopi word for a house outside a village, which seems appropriate here.

Interpretation of these ruins is a matter of educated conjecture. For example, the rock terraces at the base of Citadel Ruin appear to have been used for agricultural purposes. Likewise, the small openings in the rock wall above the entrance trail resemble arrow slits, as if they were built for defensive reasons. This would be in keeping with the Citadel's formidable location yet without supporting evidence of warfare, we cannot be sure of that interpretation.

From the mesa top, at least eight other structures are visible. This was once a populated neighborhood. Beyond the ruin is a sinkhole, the result of limestone layers collapsing beneath the surface. With a porous bottom, it was probably never a pond, nor a water source for people living here.

INDEX

Titles From FreeWheeling Travel Guides

☐ *Glacier and Waterton National Parks: A Traveler's Guide,* by Thomas Schmidt. 96 pages, $4.95

☐ *Grand Canyon: A Traveler's Guide,* by Jeremy Schmidt. 96 pages, $5.95

☐ *Yellowstone and Grand Teton National Parks: A Traveler's Guide*, by Steven Fuller and Jeremy Schmidt. 96 pages, $4.95

☐ *Yellowstone in Three Seasons,* by Steven Fuller and Jeremy Schmidt. 48 pages, 64 color photos, $6.95

☐ *The Inn at Old Faithful: An Architectural Guide,* by Susan Scofield. 32 pages, $3.75

Available from FreeWheeling Travel Guides, P.O. Box 7494, Jackson Hole, Wyoming 83001. Include $1.00 postage and handling for each title ordered.

JEREMY SCHMIDT
has lived in the Rocky Mountains for over 20 years, including seven years in Yellowstone National Park and five years near the Grand Canyon. He has written extensively on the mountain areas of the world. His book *Himalayan Passage: Seven Months in the High Country of Tibet, Nepal, China, India and Pakistan* (The Mountaineers Books, 1991) was the winner of the first Barbara Savage Memorial Award for adventure writing. Other titles include *The Rockies: Backbone of a Continent* (Thunder Bay Press, 1990), and *Adventuring in the Rockies* (Sierra Club Books, 1986).